THE ALIEN DISCLOSURE DECEPTION

The Metaphysics of Social Engineering

✳

Related Works by Charles Upton

*The System of Antichrist: Truth and Falsehood
in Postmodernism and the New Age*
(Sophia Perennis, 2001)

*Vectors of the Counter-Tradition:
The Course and Destiny of Inverted Spirituality*
(Sophia Perennis, 2012)

*Dugin against Dugin: A Traditionalist Analysis
for the Fourth Political Theory*
(Sophia Perennis, 2018)

THE ALIEN
DISCLOSURE DECEPTION

✳

The Metaphysics
of Social Engineering

CHARLES UPTON

SOPHIA PERENNIS

For information, address: Sophia Perennis
PO Box 931, Philmont, NY 12565
www.sophiaperennis.com

ISBN 978-1-59731-184-7 (pbk)

Cover design: Michael Schrauzer

Table of Contents

Introduction

The Year of the Great Disclosure?

IN THE YEAR 2021, the government of the United States has radically reversed its public stance on the reality of Unidentified Flying Objects or UFOs (now called Unidentified Aerial Phenomena) from a position of debunking or dismissal, dating from the initial reportage on the supposed crash of an alien spacecraft in Roswell, New Mexico in 1947 (which was accepted as real by the U.S. military and then debunked by them a few days later), to one of official acceptance not only of the inexplicable reality of the phenomenon but of its serious relevance to national security.

Anyone familiar with the subject, however, will be aware that this "disclosure" has actually taken place in successive stages and over a long period of time, with several national governments, including those of France and Mexico, having released their "UFO files" in recent years, as if to slowly prepare the peoples of the world for a full revelation of the "shocking truth." To take only one example, General Douglas MacArthur, in a speech to the cadets at West Point on May 12, 1962, said the following:

> We deal now, not with the things of this world alone, but with the illimitable distances and as yet unfathomed mys-

1

teries of the universe . . . of ultimate conflict between a *united human race* and *the sinister forces of some other planetary galaxy*; of such dreams and fantasies as to make life the most exciting of all times. And through all this welter of change and development your mission remains fixed, determined, inviolable. It is to win our wars.

As a contemporary example of the same kind of thinking, consider Harvard physicist Avi Loeb's proposal in "How to Avoid a Cosmic Catastrophe," an op-ed in the *Scientific American* (May 23, 2021) written from the standpoint of what has come to be called "Exopolitics" (see Parts II and III, below). According to Loeb, if an extraterrestrial civilization were to develop a "Planck collider" of sufficient size, it could generate a high-energy detonation wave or "domain wall" that would burn through the galaxy at the speed of light, destroying everything in its path. The only way to prevent this cosmic catastrophe, says Loeb, would be for earth to sign an interstellar treaty with *all* galactic civilizations capable of creating such a collider, presumably as a pledge not to build it or use it—something on the order of the nuclear test ban treaty of 1963.

Here once again, as with General MacArthur, we have the use of fear to posit the existence of one or more alien races, none of whom has yet been discovered, much less contacted, as well as of a "united human race" capable of concluding such a treaty as Dr. Loeb proposes. This is a sterling example of the virtual erasure in our time of the line between science and science-fiction, as well as of the situation described by mathematician and philosopher of science Wolfgang Smith when he wrote that "physics has lost its mind."

Introduction: The Year of the Great Disclosure?

Wild speculation based on near-zero evidence, especially when an ill-defined world of "science" is invoked as the authority for it, works to shatter consensus reality—and when people have no stable, shared worldview to believe in, such as has been traditionally provided by religion or *rational* science, they will begin to believe in just about anything offered to fill the gap. This, of course, is an ideal opportunity for the social engineers, who may in fact have brought the destruction of commonly-held worldviews to an exact science—as when the Central Intelligence Agency released LSD into the U.S. population in the 1960s. The "popularization" of earth-killing asteroids, the idea that the moon landings never took place, and the "scientific" arguments that we are all living inside a computer simulation, may represent similar engineered assaults on consensus reality.

In view of the gradual leak of mind-boggling yet ambiguous information related to UFOs over a period of 74 years (often at the hands of people with military or intelligence connections), punctuated with every brand of wild speculation, there are many indications that we have been subject to a long-term social engineering project designed according to the "gradualist" approach pioneered by the Fabian Socialists, who understood that the reliable transformation of collective beliefs and social forms is best accomplished not by violent revolution and inevitable counter-revolution but through a step-by-step agenda of attrition, seduction, and re-education.

Premier UFOlogist Jacques Vallee, for one—the model for the character of "Lacombe" in Steven Spielberg's movie "Close Encounters of the Third Kind"—put forth this possibility in his book *Messengers of Deception* (1979). The present book contains a speculative history of this kind of social engineering project in the United States since the end of World War II.

The UFO phenomenon cannot however simply be limited to a massive hoax of the "Mission Impossible" sort, since it is based on a real phenomenon (inexplicable according to our present understanding of the laws of physics) which is characterized both by undeniable physical evidence and by equally undeniable psychic and psychological effects that can only be described as "paranormal."

If we consider the *physical* evidence alone, we will be led to conjecture that we are being visited by physical spacecraft from other planets piloted by the kind of sentient beings presently termed "aliens," "ETs" (extra-terrestrials), or "EBEs" (extraterrestrial biological entities).

If we consider the *psychic* evidence alone, we may conclude that we are in the presence of mental illness, either individual or collective (whether or not it is being deliberately engineered), or of symbolic visionary experiences (this is what Carl Jung believed), or else of the activities of non-material spiritual entities.

And if we consider both physical and psychic evidence *simultaneously*, we may come to some much more interesting conclusions. But if the UFO aliens are real, and if they exhibit both physical and psychic aspects, what becomes of the whole "social engineering" theory? From my point-of-view, this is the most interesting question of all, one that I attempt to answer as thoroughly as possible in this book by applying criteria from five sources: traditional metaphysics and eschatology; psychology; the physical sciences; the well-attested phenomenology of the paranormal from many sources; and socio-historical analysis.

Since the global ruling classes, or their hired "experts" at least, are entirely conversant with all these areas of research and development, and have learned how to apply them to the control and transformation of societies over a period of many generations, *I believe those of us who still hope to preserve elements of our freedom and human dignity in these extremely dark times need to become at least as well-informed on these matters as our implacable adversaries.*

✳

This book is an anthology of my writings from 2001 until the present (revised to better reflect current political events related directly to Disclosure) dealing with the subject of UFOs, beginning with Chapter Seven of my book *The System of Antichrist: Truth and Falsehood in Postmodernism and the New Age* (Sophia Perennis, 2001), entitled "The UFO Phenomenon, a Postmodern Demonology"— which, in 2005, with the addition of the sections "Preliminaries" and "Memoir and Conclusion," became the short book *Cracks in the Great Wall: The UFO Phenomenon and Traditional Metaphysics* (Sophia Perennis, 2005). This material constitutes Part I of the present book. Part II draws upon Chapter Six of my book *Vectors of the Counter-Initiation: The Course and Destiny of Inverted Spirituality* (Sophia Perennis, 2012), again brought into line with current events. Part III is an article I wrote in 2018 and recently updated to carry my argument as far as this pivotal year of 2021. Parts IV and V were written in this year, as was Jonathan Solvie's Appendix I and my Appendix II. I found no reason to revise the conclusions I came to in 2001 regarding the real nature of UFOs and the deception activities surrounding them, since in fact I still hold to these conclusions; as of 2021, I see nothing that needs to be changed. Beyond that, whatever elements were originally offered as contemporary reportage in my earlier writings are still entirely valid and useful as history, and may be especially interesting under present circumstances. The analysis I composed in 2012, which makes up Part II of this book, demonstrates how work was being done as early as the 1940s toward both the propagation of a *mass belief* in the "reality" of UFOs, and the placement of this belief in a specific context designed to further certain social engineering goals. This artificially-created worldview, so long in the making, is now being been further vindicated, and further *imposed*, by the "Great Disclosure" of 2021. Whether this disclosure will produce a newly-established sense of certainty, or simply deepen the contradictions and ambiguities we have been subjected to over the past 74 years, remains to be seen.

In this book I believe I have accomplished three things: First, to explain the nature of UFOs as a primary phenomenon on the basis of traditional metaphysics, eschatology and demonology; secondly, to trace the development of the UFO *myth* as a contemporary belief system, whether it takes the form of a set of quasi-scientific speculations or a pseudo-religion or both; third, to uncover some of the history of the various human deception activities that have grown up around it, especially since World War II, while carrying on informed speculation as to their nature, methods and possible goals.

✳

One of the vices that appears on the traditional Christian list of the Seven Deadly Sins is *accidia*, or Sloth. Sloth is a complicated sin. It is not simply laziness but also includes despondency, fear, distraction, complacency, irresponsibility, procrastination, cowardice, daydreaming, making lame excuses—whatever prevents you from *acting* when the Call comes in to act. Sloth is inseparable from a condition of oppression or "lockdown"; it is a sign of what Paulo Freire, in his classic *The Pedagogy of the Oppressed*, called "internalized oppression." Oppressed people become slothful because they believe that all effective action is impossible; likewise Sloth is oppressive in itself because it destroys the *one-pointedness* necessary for both penetrating insight and a vigorous and committed response to what insight has discovered; people who feel that "nothing can be done" will also likely believe that "nothing can be known."

In compiling this book it was Sloth more than anything else that I had to struggle against. When I asked my wife why she thought that an uncritical acceptance of the increasingly "official" explanation for the UFO phenomenon would produce a state of Sloth, her answer was: "Because it prevents us from defending the human world we have inherited." It is my hope that all who accept the value of their human dignity will take this book seriously, whether or not they agree with everything in it (which they likely will not), and then rise to the defense of that dignity, against the whole spectrum of inhuman forces, ideas, and influences that menace us in the twenty-first century—as well as against the human agents who enforce them—with all deliberate speed.

✳

A Note to the Reader

*To restate my thesis as simply as possible, I believe there is compelling evidence that apparitions of UFOs and their "alien" occupants are paranormal events. There are also many signs of human deception surrounding this phenomenon. However, these two bodies of evidence **do not depend on each other**; the reader who cannot easily accept the paranormal explanation is free to set aside any arguments that rely on such arcane beliefs and consider the evidence I have presented for human deception activities—particularly in Part V—on its own merits. Whether UFOs are hoaxes, misunderstood natural phenomena, artefacts of unknown human technology, examples of extraterrestrial technology, or occult manifestations, there are clear indications that the phenomenon is being used as a basis for one or more social engineering agendas, **whether or not the directors of these agendas know what UFOs actually are**. I hope the reader will keep this in mind while moving through the several different perspectives on the UFO phenomenon presented in this book.*

Part I

The UFO Phenomenon
&
Traditional Metaphysics

*

Cracks in the Great Wall

The UFO Phenomenon
&
Traditional Metaphysics

Cracks in the Great Wall

[Including, But Not Limited to, the UFO Phenomenon and the Deception Activities Surrounding It as of 2001/2005]

Preliminaries

AT THE PRESENT TIME the attempt to understand the UFO phenomenon seems to be going around in circles. The hypothesis that they are spaceships from other planets, the idea that they could be manifestations of "fairies" or "spirit-entities," and the suspicion that they may represent part of a government-sponsored mass mind-control program, chase each other in a maddening spiral, to no clear end. Much energy is expended in trying to make the Federal government "come clean about what it knows," but as UFOlogist Jacques Vallee has observed, the government is most likely covering up nothing but its own ignorance. Undoubtedly it has many more reports of the phenomenon in its archives than have been released to the public, but whether our wise rulers have been able to make any real sense of them is far from certain—though it is certainly in their interest to let us believe they have. The belief that their "intelligence capabilities" stretch far beyond this planet, that the military-industrial priesthood is in touch with mysterious beings from beyond the stars, beings who possess fantastically advanced technologies, is certainly useful in order to subdue and terrorize the citizenry. [NOTE: *The 2021 "disclosure" that the government accepts the UFO phenomenon as "real" but of undetermined nature and origin is certainly not the end of the matter. It has simply set the stage for more intense speculation, from many quarters—official, un-official and semi-official—as to what the phenomenon actually is, as well as further calls for the government and the scientific community to reveal what they "really" know.*] "Area 51" may or may not be a testing-ground for arcane, possibly "psychotronic" technologies, but there is no question of its usefulness for social engineering. The intelligence community undoubtedly derives a great deal of valuable data from observing the myths and rituals related to Nevada's "Dreamland" generated by a frightened and mystified populace.

With hope for meaningful closure on the true nature of the phenomenon fading [*as of 2005*], those who have spent years pursuing such closure with little success have either sunk into a stunned, bitter cynicism about what has in some cases been their life's quest—a cynicism which fits right in with our contemporary "postmodern" cynicism about the possibility of arriving at *any* kind of objective truth—or have opted instead for a worship of mystification itself, based on the feeling that if true mysteries still exist in this oppressive, modern, scientific world, things that not even science or the government can explain, then there is still "hope"—a hope that would disappear if the phenomenon were ever really understood. And so the quest to explain the UFO mystery becomes gradually and unwittingly transformed into the need to maintain it at any cost: "The truth is out there—please don't let it get any nearer." What started as a burning desire to explain the phenomenon thereby ends up as an active (though unconscious) resistance to the kind of comprehensive and adequate explanation which I believe this book provides. To fascinate oneself with mysterious happenings may be entertaining, but it is also addictive, and ultimately ruinous to one's psychic health. If knowledge is possible, then it is always better to know.

The reason we find it so difficult to understand the UFO phenomenon is because we no longer apprehend the full structure of being. Earlier cultures understood, and every world religion still teaches, that material reality is only the lowest level of a universe composed of material, psychic, spiritual, and Divine domains. In the words of the late Fr Malachi Martin, from a letter to me in response to an earlier draft of some of this material, "precisely it is a question of metaphysical knowledge lacking that has queered the pitch for an understanding of what has been happening." Science has a great deal to teach us about material reality, a certain modest amount to teach us about psychic reality, and nothing at all to teach us about spiritual reality. Therefore no scientist, if he limits himself to science as it is presently defined, can give a comprehensive explanation of UFOs. Nor can psychic researchers and "ghost busters" ultimately clear up the mystery. Both can make valuable contributions, but unless their findings are seen in the light of metaphysics, particularly traditional metaphysics, no closure can be reached. Nowadays the word "metaphysics" conjures up images of ghosts, witches, spirit-entities, and—UFOs. Traditional metaphysics, however, is philosophy, often esoteric or mystical philosophy. Plato, Plotinus (Greeks) Shankara (Hindu), Nagarjuna (Buddhist), Ibn al-Arabi and Rumi (Muslims), Dionysius the Areopagite, Maximos the Confessor, Meister Eckhart and Dante Alighieri (Christians) were practitioners of traditional metaphysics.

When writing on traditional metaphysics, I draw largely on the writers of the Traditionalist or Perennialist School: René Guénon, A. K. Coomaraswamy, Frithjof Schuon, Titus Burckhardt, Martin Lings, Huston Smith, Rama Coomaraswamy, Wolfgang Smith, Joseph Epes Brown, Leo Schaya, Marco Pallis, Whitall Perry, James Cutsinger, S. H. Nasr, etc. And probably the writer most useful in helping us understand what UFOs are from the metaphysical perspective is René Guénon, who (along with Ananda Coomaraswamy) is usually considered to be the "founder" of the Traditionalist School. [*His name has been associated with American politico Steve Bannon in recent years as one of Bannon's influences.*] Guénon, who died in 1950, investigated almost every occult or pseudo-esoteric group available to him in his native France before and after WWI: Spiritualists, Theosophists, Martinists, Neo-Gnostics, to name only a few. He emerged from his tour through the occult underworld of his time with an understanding that these groups were not simply childish and wrong-headed, but actively destructive to social stability and spiritual truth. At the same time, under the tutelage of fully-qualified teachers, he was studying the real teachings of the Hindu Vedanta, esoteric Taoism and Islamic Sufism as no one had ever done before in the Western world, at least in modern times, and rigorously separating them from the many fantastic and distorted ideas attributed to these eastern religions by various western occultists, notably those of the Theosophical Society. His ability to distinguish valid, comprehensive esoteric doctrines from the spurious concoctions of the occultists revealed to him the existence of what he called "the agents of the Counter-Initiation." He saw that behind many occult groups, largely populated by sincere but deluded spiritual dreamers, lurked much more sinister forces, forces consciously dedicated to the destruction of all true spiritualities, both exoteric and esoteric—even initiatory ones.

Guénon's writing stretched from profound expositions of "pure" metaphysics and the doctrines of eastern religions to exposés of many aspects of western occultism and the various subversive and secret societies through which it operated—and continues to. And his prophetic masterpiece, in which he brought these two poles together, is *The Reign of Quantity and the Signs of the Times*, which becomes more relevant with each passing year. In this work he reveals the Counter-Initiation to be a precursor of the regime of the Antichrist, and its ultimate goal nothing less than the dissolution of the present world. A large part of what I have tried to do in the present book is to look at the UFO phenomenon—largely as presented by that most reliable and comprehensive of UFOlogists, Jacques Vallee—through the lens of traditional metaphysics, particularly that of Guénon's *Reign of Quantity*.

Another of Guénon's books is also valuable, however, for the historical light it throws on the belief in "aliens" and UFOs. In *The Spiritist Fallacy*, Guénon shows how many twentieth-century Spiritualists believed that discarnate spirits occupy space. He quotes one Ernest Bosc as calling them "our friends in Space," in response to an article in the Spiritualist magazine *Fraternist* published in 1913. It may be significant that, fifty-five years later, the hippies were calling extra-terrestrials "space brothers," and the New Age movement since the '70s has all but erased the distinction between space aliens and discarnate spirits.

Guénon mentions, as an example of the inflated pretensions of American Spiritualists, a group calling itself the "Ancient Order of Melchizedek." He also speaks of an "Esoteric Fraternity" in Boston led by the blind Hiram Butler.

Interestingly enough, this same Order of Melchizedek, as well as Hiram Butler—who also, as it turns out, established a group by the same name in California in 1889, on a communal farm in the foothills of the Sierras—make their appearance in *Messengers of Deception* (1979), by UFO researcher Jacques Vallee. Vallee investigated several groups, both in France and in the United States, calling themselves the Order of Melchizedek, and described the figure of Melchizedek, Abraham's master from the book of Genesis who had neither father or mother, as "a symbol and a rallying point for saucer contactees." So it seems possible that the widespread belief in UFOs, if not the proliferation of the phenomenon itself, are among the social and psychological fruits of the Spiritualist movement of the late nineteenth and early twentieth centuries, which is in so many ways the direct ancestor of the New Age movement of today.

In *The Spiritist Fallacy*, Guénon has this to say:

> [What] we see . . . in spiritism and other analogous movements, are influences that incontestably come from what some have called the "sphere of the Antichrist." This designation can also be taken symbolically, but that changes nothing in reality and does not render the influences less ill-omened. Assuredly, those who participate in such movements, and even those who believe they direct them, may know nothing of these things. This is where the greatest danger lies, for quite certainly many of them would flee in horror if they knew they were servants of the "powers of darkness." But their blindness is often irremediable and their good faith even helps draw in other victims. Does not this allow us to say that the supreme craft of the devil, however he may be conceived, is to make us deny his existence?[1]

As the reader will discover, I consider the contemporary UFO experience, and particularly the occurrence of "alien abduction," to be the most direct manifestation conceivable of these powers of darkness—a manifestation which has become possible on such a widespread basis only because the present world-age is rapidly drawing toward a close: it is truly an "end time" phenomenon. To demonstrate this, I have made use not only of the writings of René Guénon and Jacques Vallee, but also those of C.S. Lewis, Seraphim Rose, Frithjof Schuon, Whitall Perry, and Leo Schaya, with whose help I believe I have put together the most comprehensive and definitive explanation of the

---

[1] *The Spiritist Fallacy* (Hillsdale, NY: Sophia Perennis, 2004), 276.

UFO phenomenon available today—though if anybody else can do better, then more power to him (or her); no one holds, or should hope to hold, the copyright on truth.

UFOs and
Traditional Metaphysics

WHEN ASKED to define "reality," William James gave the following answer: "Anything is real which we find ourselves obliged to take account of in any way." According to this broad (though far from deep) definition, UFOs are certainly real, and mass belief in them has had an immense effect upon our society. Nor has this belief simply materialized out of nothing; there is method behind this social, psychic, and empirically documented madness.

Friedrich Nietzsche said "Be careful: while you are looking into the abyss, the abyss is also looking into you." This is why I caution the reader not to delve into this book while in a state of depression, anxiety, or morbid curiosity. Whoever already knows how bad UFOs are, and is not required by his or her duties to investigate them, should ignore this information. Those who think there may be something "spiritual" in them, however, and are not afraid of being seriously disillusioned, should read on.

The Place of the UFO Myth in
Contemporary Culture

The UFO phenomenon constitutes a true postmodern demonology—though all too many of those who believe that Unidentified Flying Objects are extraterrestrial visitors treat it more as a postmodern religion. And this religious or quasi-religious relationship to the phenomenon is certainly not limited to the UFO cults *per se*. To take only one example: according to UFO researcher Jacques Vallee, in his *Messengers of Deception*,[2] the "pope" and founder of the Church of Scientology L. Ron Hubbard—who died in 1986 and who, according to my late '60s correspondence with ex-Scientologist William Burroughs, had a background in Naval Intelligence—"is said to have practiced ritual magic with a rocket expert named Jack Parsons, who met in the Mojave Desert in 1945 a 'Spiritual Being' he regarded as a Venusian." According to Vallee, both Hubbard and Parsons had a background in the Ordo Templi Orientis, founded by black magician and British Intelligence asset Aleister Crowley. Parsons, however, went on to become co-founder of both the Aerojet Corporation and the Jet Propulsion Laboratory.

Whether true or false, such assertions are right in line with the contemporary UFO folklore, which informs us that our modern technology is either a "gift" of the saucer-people or a product of back-engineering from the saucer that supposedly crashed in Roswell, New Mexico in 1947. Such beliefs are to be found not only among New Age cults or eccentric hermits living in camping trailers; many "responsible" and well-established computer professionals, and even corporate executives of our "information culture," also hold them. For example, Joe Firmage, CEO of US Web/CKS, the two billion dollar internet marketing

---

[2] *Messengers of Deception* (Berkeley: And/Or Press, 1979).

and consulting firm he created, quit that position in 2000 to spread the UFO gospel. And at least one U.S. President, Jimmy Carter, admits to having witnessed a UFO. Ideas once the province of the "lunatic fringe" are now increasingly acceptable among the political and corporate elite. So at the very least we can say that UFO mythology is on its way to becoming socially dominant, or at least highly significant, in today's global society—something mythographer Joseph Campbell was well aware of when he became "mythic advisor" to George Lucas for his *Star Wars* trilogy.

The fact that I've had to delve deeply into traditional metaphysics in order to deal with the UFO phenomenon from a stable intellectual standpoint, and to criticize such beliefs as "physical" time-travel and literal human reincarnation when dealing with the myth of "aliens," shows the degree to which ideas René Guénon called "counter-initiatory" have occupied the centers of human consciousness that have been abandoned over the past few centuries by traditional metaphysics and theology. According to Guénon in his prophetic work *The Reign of Quantity and the Signs of the Times,* as this cycle of manifestation draws to a close, the cosmic environment first solidifies—this being in a way both the result and the cause of modern materialism—after which it simply fractures, because a material reality absolutely cut off from subtler planes of being is metaphysically impossible.

These cracks in the "great wall" separating the physical universe from the subtle or animic plane initially open in a "downward" direction, toward the "infra-psychic" or demonic realm [cf. Rev. 9:1–3]; "magical realism" replaces "ordinary life." It is only at the final moment that a great crack opens in the "upward" direction, at the Second Coming of Christ, the advent of that Being whom the Hindus call the Kalki Avatara, who will bring this world to a close and inaugurate the next cycle of manifestation. And yet, for those with faith in God and an intuition of the Absolute, the "upward crack," since it opens onto Eternity, is here already. Although the mass mind is becoming less and less able to see it, the Door of Grace is not closed: "Behold I am with you all days, even unto the consummation of the age." As the dark shadow of a greater Light than this world can produce, the UFO phenomenon is no less than an eschatological sign.

There is no question that the UFO myth has deeply affected the mass mind. When the Heaven's Gate cult committed group suicide near San Diego in the March of 1997, the question of the place of UFO ideology in contemporary life became, for a short time, the most compelling question confronting the American people. The followers of M.H. Applewhite, who were also avid *Star Trek* fans, apparently believed that their souls would be reunited after death aboard a "spaceship" that was invisibly following the Hale-Bopp comet. At the autopsy of the cult members, it was discovered that some of the males had been castrated, an operation later claimed to have been voluntary.

There are some truths that it is shameful to know; the truth about UFOs is one of them. Even fifty years ago, such knowledge could only be encountered by someone pathologically attracted to human degeneracy and the dark side of the spiritual world. But today, what used to be the province of a few black magicians cannot be entirely avoided by any of us.

The UFO phenomenon is perhaps the most sinister complex of beliefs and events to be found among those loosely associated with the New Age. It has emerged from the shadows of pop science fiction and fringe occultism to become part of "mainstream" American culture, as a belief-system or cultural "archetype" if not a personal experience. The popular *X-Files* TV series, and the flood of "New Age" books and publications that present teachings supposedly given by "aliens"—*The Pleiadian Agenda* by Barbara Hand Clow, for example—are proof enough. In order to make sense of the phenomenon, I will waste no time in speculating whether or not it really is, or could be, occurring, but will simply accept the conclusions of reliable researchers in the field, notably Dr Jacques Vallee, and proceed from there. I will also accept, without apology, the existence of invisible worlds, and the ability of such worlds to impinge upon and alter the physical one. As Frithjof Schuon says,

> However restricted the experience of modern man may be in things belonging to the psychic or subtle order, there are still phenomena of that kind which are in no way inaccessible to him in principle, but he treats them from the start as "superstitions" and hands them over to the occultists. Acceptance of the psychic dimension is in any case part of religion: one cannot deny magic without straying from faith.[3]

It is traditional Catholic doctrine, for example, to teach the reality of magic and witchcraft, so that the faithful will be

[3] *Light on the Ancient Worlds* (Bloomington, IN: World Wisdom Books, 1984), 104.

sure to avoid them. I would only add that where modern man denies the reality of psychic phenomena, postmodern man accepts them all too easily, then uses them to rebel against religion, and finally to supplant God.

To face the spiritual darkness which the UFO phenomenon represents and not be damaged, a kind of double consciousness is needed. To begin with, we will have to admit that such things as alien "landings" and human "abductions" are actually taking place. But we also need to remember that, as James Cutsinger says, "there is a greater degree of Being in the beautiful than in the ugly."[4] In the words of Schuon:

> Nothingness "is" not, but it "appears" with respect to the real, as the real projects itself toward the finite. To move away from the Divine Principle is to become "other than He," while remaining of necessity in Him, since He is the sole reality. This means that the world necessarily comprises—in a relative fashion, of course, since nothingness does not exist—that privation of reality or of perfection which we call "evil." On the one hand, evil does not come from God, since, being negative, it cannot have any positive cause; on the other, evil results from the unfolding of Divine manifestation, but in this respect, precisely, it is not "evil," it is simply the shadow of a process which is positive in itself.

> Finally, if we consider in *Maya* [i.e., Divine manifestation conceived of as having a partly illusory nature, of not being what it seems] the quality of "obscurity" or "ignorance" (*tamas*) as it is manifested in nature in general or man in particular, we are compelled to see in it what

---

[4] *Advice to the Serious Seeker: Meditations on the Teachings of Frithjof Schuon* (Albany: SUNY, 1997), 34.

might be called the "mystery of absurdity"; the absurd is that which, in itself and not as regards its metaphysical cause, is deprived of sufficient reason and manifests no more than its own blind accidentality. The genesis of the world in the first place, and the unfolding of human events, appear as a struggle against absurdity; the intelligible is confirmed as a contrast to the unintelligible.[5]

In other words, evil is like a hole in Being. In a sense, it actually exists—you'd better not deny this, or you'll fall into the hole! But in another sense, it isn't real, since it is nothing but a lack or diminishment of reality, an empty space. The world of UFOs is like a waking nightmare, a world of dark unrealities made actual. But if we remember that beauty is more real than ugliness, and that Reality is good in essence, then we can—with God's help—look ugliness in the face and not be conquered by it, not finally *convinced*. Because, as Schuon says, even though evil in its own nature is ultimately unreal, we still have to struggle against it. According to Schuon's pure metaphysics, evil is a product of that inevitable motion of Being away from its Divine Principle which manifests as the cosmos. Just as light is always leaving the Sun *because* the Sun is radiant, shining ever more dimly into the surrounding darkness, so the very fact that God is not only Absolute but Infinite means that His Being must communicate itself, must eternally radiate in the direction of a Non-Being, which however can never be reached because it exists only as a tendency, not as a "real" part of Being. But the fact that, as Schuon says, we have to struggle against the constant pull of absurdity and Non-Being means that the doctrine of

---

[5] *Logic and Transcendence* (NY: Harper & Row, 1975), 154–55.

evil derived from his pure metaphysics must be balanced by the complementary *theological* doctrine that evil is always the product of an abuse of free will, by men or by spiritual beings. This apparent contradiction is resolved by the mysterious identity of choice and destiny, without which God's knowledge of our destiny would negate our freedom, rather than being His eternal and present knowledge of how we decide to use that freedom. And the fact that evil is "unintelligible" does not mean that there is no order or method in it; if it were "pure" chaos, it would not exist in even a relative sense. So evil cannot be absolutely unintelligible. It is better to describe it as *motion in the direction of* an absolute unintelligibility which, as pure Non-Being, can never be reached. Therefore, any organization or design that may appear within evil is not part of its own nature, but has been stolen by evil from the Good. This is why true evil always exhibits a tell-tale mixture of diabolical cunning and immense stupidity.

✳

In the first half of the twentieth century the dominant image of extraterrestrials was of horrible monsters from other worlds arriving on earth in spaceships to conquer and destroy. The representative book of this phase was H.G. Wells' *War of the Worlds*, published in 1898, which might almost be taken as prophetic of the First World War, when tanks, flame-throwers, poison gas, and aerial bombardment first shocked the world with the horrors of technological warfare. The power of this myth over the collective mind was amply demonstrated by Orson Welles' "War of the Worlds" radio hoax in 1938 on the eve of

World War II. (I've always been struck by the fact that both men had nearly the same last name; something was definitely "welling up" from the psychic underworld...)

This image of extraterrestrials as inhuman monsters is still with us. But in the late 1950s it began to be supplemented by a radically different myth, that of the wise and powerful extraterrestrials who come to earth to save us from nuclear self-destruction. The famous motion picture starring Michael Rennie, *The Day the Earth Stood Still* (1951), is the representative expression of this idea, which became the view of extraterrestrials dominant in the hippy movement. The hippy belief, appearing the second half of the '60s and inherited by the New Age movement some time in the '70s, had to do with the Space Brothers of the Intergalactic Council—in many ways the folk version of the United Federation of Planets from the *Star Trek* television series—who were either here to save the earth, or else to take all the good hippies away with them to a better world in a counterculture adaptation of the Evangelical Christian doctrine of "the rapture." And the "Mothership" that was supposed to be hovering invisibly overhead waiting to receive them was (in my opinion) a distorted version of the Heavenly Jerusalem. The most detailed written expression of this belief-system was and is a massive "channeled" text, *The Book of Urantia* (1955); the myth of the benign extraterrestrial was also the basis of motion pictures like *Close Encounters of the Third Kind* (1977) and *ET* (1982).

Things began to change around the time Whitley Strieber's sinister book *Communion* was published in 1986. With increasing numbers of reported "alien abductions" (according to a 1991 survey, between several hundred thousand and several *million* Americans believe that they've been victims of such events), the concept of the benign Space Brother slowly began to be replaced by that of the demonic kidnapper, just as the cartoon cliché of the little green man with antennae on his head was turning into that of the "gray": the corpse-colored, hairless being with huge, black, elongated eyes—an image derived directly from Strieber's descriptions as depicted on the cover of his book. (UFO researcher Jacques Vallee describes this image as "wise and benign"; but to me it is bone-chilling.)

I saw Strieber interviewed once on a PBS documentary. He admitted that his encounters with aliens were the most horrible events of his life, but showed absolutely *no desire to break with them* on this account. The encounters were so strange and compelling that his fascination for them outweighed all other considerations—including, apparently, his own self-respect. I was reminded of the situation of the abused wife or incested child who can't imagine life apart from his or her abuser. It is a psychological truth that any extremely intense experience becomes in a sense "numinous." We tend to identify the most powerful things that have ever happened to us with "reality" itself. The daughter raped by her father will carry this experience in her psyche as an indelible reference point, which in later life may lead her to demonize and/or idealize other men in whom she sees, or upon whom she projects, aspects of her father. The soldier brutalized in war will seek out other violent situations—perhaps even making his living as a mercenary—because even though he knows that "war is hell," he can't let it alone. "Normal life" situations seem empty and unreal to him; nowhere but in the presence of bloody violence is he entirely "himself." He left part of his soul back on the battlefield and keeps returning to the place where he lost it. Only at the scene of the original crime does he feel, for a moment at least, complete.

The Place of UFOs in the Hierarchy of Being

According to traditional metaphysics, as we have seen above, Being is arranged hierarchically, in discrete ontological levels. This is the "Great Chain of Being" of the eighteenth century, which, when it "collapsed"—when, that is, we started to see the hierarchy of Being horizontally in terms of time instead of vertically in terms of eternity—was transformed into the myth of *progress*. When we no longer recognized the Absolute as the eternal crown of the hierarchy of Being, we were forced to imagine that something bigger and better—or at least weirder and more powerful—lies in the Future. "God *above*" is replaced by "whatever is going to happen up *ahead*." All spiritual traditions and traditional philosophies include the Great Chain of Being in one form or another, but since every metaphysician seems to render it a little differently, I'll take the risk of presenting my own version of it, which probably owes more to Sufi theosopher Ibn al-'Arabi and Traditionalist metaphysician Frithjof Schuon than to anyone else, but can't strictly be attributed to either of them. It is based on eight levels of Being, in descending order. Each level not only transcends all that is below it, but also contains, in higher form, all that is below it. The first two levels are purely divine, the second two spiritual, the third two psychic, and the fourth two physical.

The Divine

The *first* level is Beyond Being (Dionysius the Areopagite), the Godhead (Meister Eckhart), the unknowable Divine Essence.

The *second* level is pure Being, Allah, the "Deity," God Himself—the personal God Who is Creator, Ruler, Judge, and Savior of the universe, while transcending these functions absolutely, since He is not limited by any relationship with created Being.

The Spirit

The *third* level is the Intellect, God's primal act of Self-understanding in terms of subject and object—in Christian terms, "God the Father" and "God the Son" (though, strictly speaking, Christian theology sees the Father and the Son as Divine Persons, and thus as aspects of the *second* level, above). Intellect is the ray of the Divine within the creatures—the *nous* of the Neo-Platonic philosophers —about which Eckhart said, "there is Something in the soul which is uncreated and uncreatable." In terms of its creative function, the Intellect is the *pneuma*, the Holy Spirit of God that "moved upon the face of the waters."

The *fourth* level is the Archangelic, the realm of the permanent archetypes or Divine Names, perhaps represented by the Seven Lamps and the Four Living Creatures surrounding the Throne of the Lamb in the *Apocalypse*. This is the level of the eternal metaphysical principles or Platonic Ideas, which, far from being abstractions, are in reality more densely concrete (for all their transparency to the Divine Light) and more highly charged with creative and truth-revealing energy than anything below them.

The Psyche

The *fifth* level is the Angelic, the manifestation of the Spirit on the psychic plane, the plane of thought, emotion and intent. Each angel is both a living, conscious individual and the manifestation of a specific Idea.

The *sixth* level is the Imaginal, the "astral plane" or *alam al-mithal*, where every thought, feeling, or intent, whatever the level of being it essentially corresponds to, appears as a symbolic image that is at the same time a living being. This is the world of dreams and mental images, which is not simply happening inside this or that individual consciousness, but is continuous with an objective psychic "environment," just as the human body is continuous with the natural world.

The Material World

The *seventh* level is the Etheric. This is the realm of the "soul of matter," the hidden face of nature, the world of the Celtic *Fairies*, the Muslim *Jinn*, the world of "bioplasma," of auras, of elemental spirits, and subtle energies. It is the World Soul, the essential pattern and subtle substance of the material world.

The *eighth* level is the Material, the world reported by our senses. Science deals almost exclusively with the eighth level, though it must sometimes confront phenomena emanating from the seventh, and theorize about seventh-level realities in order to explain apparent paradoxes appearing on the eighth. And since science has largely replaced religion and metaphysics as our dominant way of looking at the world, we are at nearly a total loss when it comes to explaining, and especially to *evaluating*, the

UFO phenomenon. Because we believe in evolution and progress instead of understanding the eternal hierarchical nature of Being, *anything* that pops through from level seven to level eight, as far as we are concerned, might be God, or Merlin the Magician, or a "highly-evolved technological race," or God knows what. And the reason why so many seventh-level beings are now appearing to us on a global level may be *because* we have lost the ability to evaluate them; they can now represent themselves to us as anything they please.

Who the "Aliens" Are

According to Muslim doctrine, the Jinn—plural of "Jinni," the well-known spook from the lamp—are beings inhabiting a plane subtler than the Material but grosser than the Imaginal and Angelic: the *seventh* plane in the Great Chain of Being.

"Aliens" are members of the Jinn. According to Jacques Vallee, the most balanced and reliable of UFO researchers, who was invited to present his findings at a closed conference with U.N. General Secretary Kurt Waldheim (as recounted in his *Messengers of Deception*, which everyone interested in the UFO phenomenon should read), the phenomenon has three aspects. (1) It is a real, and inexplicable, phenomenon that appears on radar and leaves real physical traces. (2) It is a psychic phenomenon that profoundly affects people's perceptions. (3) It is surrounded by deceptions of the "Mission Impossible" variety produced by actual human groups, apparently for the purpose of affecting mass belief.

But how can we possibly put these three facts together? If UFOs are physically real, we say, they must be spaceships. If they are psychic, they must either be the product of mass hysteria, or real psychic entities. But if they are "staged," how can they be either? The mind grapples for closure. If they are spaceships, we must turn to astronomy, NASA and the Defense Department for information on them. If they are subtle entities, the psychics will tell us what they are up to. And if they are staged events, we must rely on counter-intelligence and investigative reporting. *But if they are all three...???* The critical mind tries to make sense of this, fails, and shuts down. It is meant to.

Father Seraphim Rose, an American-born Eastern Orthodox priest who died in 1982, gives perhaps the best explanation of the UFO phenomenon we possess: simply put, they are demons. They do what demons have always done. Their "craft" are products of a demonic "technology" that begins in the subtle realm and impinges on this one. He writes:

> The most puzzling aspect of UFO phenomena to most researchers—namely, the strange mingling of physical and psychic characteristics in them—is no puzzle at all to readers of Orthodox spiritual books, especially the *Lives of the Saints*. Demons also have "physical bodies," although the "matter" in them is of such subtlety that it cannot be perceived by men unless their spiritual "doors of perception" are opened, whether with God's will (in the case of holy men) or against it (in the case of sorcerers and mediums).
>
> Orthodox literature has many examples of demonic manifestations which fit precisely the UFO pattern: apparitions of "solid" beings and objects (whether demons themselves or their illusory creations) which suddenly

"materialize" and "dematerialize," always with the aim of awing and confusing people and ultimately leading them to perdition. The *Lives* of the fourth-century St Anthony the Great and the third-century St Cyprian the Former Sorcerer are filled with such incidents. . . .

It is clear that the manifestations of today's "flying saucers" are quite within the "technology" of demons; indeed, nothing else can explain them as well. The multifarious demonic deceptions of Orthodox literature have been adapted to the mythology of outer space, nothing more... [their] purpose [is] to awe the beholders with a sense of the "mysterious," and to produce "proof" of the "higher intelligences" ("angels," if the victim believes in them, or "space visitors" for modern men), and thereby to gain trust for the *message* they wish to communicate.[6]

And lest the reader assume that only a traditional Christian monk could gain this impression, Fr Seraphim quotes from the introduction to *UFOs and Related Subjects: An Annotated Bibliography,*[7] prepared by the Library of Congress for the United States Air Force Office of Scientific Research:

Many of the UFO reports now being published in the popular press recount alleged incidents that are strikingly similar to demonic possession and psychic phenomena which have long been known to theologians and parapsychologists.[8]

Fr Seraphim, writing in the 1970s, relates the UFO phenomenon to the attraction of our culture as a whole to sci-

[6] *Orthodoxy and the Religion of the Future* (Platina, CA: St Herman of Alaska Brotherhood, 1975), 134, 136.

[7] By Lynn G. Catoe (Washington, DC: US Government Printing Office, 1969).

[8] *Orthodoxy and the Religion of the Future,* 132.

ence fiction—a point driven home in 1997 when the Heaven's Gate cult, after committing mass suicide, were revealed as computer-savvy "trekkies." He writes:

> The future world and humanity are seen by science fiction ostensibly in terms of "projections" from present-day scientific discoveries; in actuality, however, these "projections" correspond quite remarkably to the everyday reality of occult and overtly demonic experience throughout the ages. Among the characteristics of the "highly evolved" creatures of the future are: communication by mental telepathy, ability to fly, materialize and dematerialize, transform the appearances of things or create illusionary scenes and creatures by "pure thought," travel at speeds far beyond any modern technology, to take possession of the bodies of earthmen; and the expounding of a "spiritual" philosophy which is "beyond all religions" and holds promise of a state where "advanced intelligences" will no longer be dependent upon matter. All these are standard practices and claims of sorcerers and demons. A recent history of science fiction notes that "a persistent aspect of the vision of science fiction is the desire to transcend normal experience . . . through the presentation of characters and events that transgress the conditions of space and time as we know them" (Robert Scholes and Eric S. Rabkin, *Science Fiction: History, Science, Vision*. Oxford University Press, 1977, 175). The scripts of *Star Trek* and other science fiction stories, with their futuristic "scientific" devices, read in parts like excerpts from the lives of the ancient Orthodox Saints, where the actions of sorcerers are described at a time when sorcery was still a strong part of pagan life.[9]

Fr Seraphim Rose repeats Jacques Vallee's hypothesis that UFOs "are constructed *both as physical craft and as*

[9] Ibid., 103–4.

psychic devices." He also accepts Vallee's conclusion, based on a statistical analysis of only those sightings that are most convincing, that they can't be interplanetary spaceships because there are simply too many of them; it is not likely, for example, that the possibly two million Americans who have been abducted by aliens were kidnapped by astronauts. (Dr Vallee, as an astronomer, statistician, and computer scientist, is well equipped to carry on this kind of analysis.) Fr Seraphim doesn't entirely explain Vallee's hard evidence for deception activities traceable to human groups, though his comparison of UFO phenomena to those produced by the sorcerers of antiquity is highly suggestive.

My own depressing hypothesis is this: Various groups of occultists or black magicians bent on world domination, some of whom seem to have ties with the intelligence community (see Vallee, *Messengers of Deception*, and *Revelations*),[10] and who may or may not possess "inter-dimensional" technologies provided or inspired by the Jinn, are staging deceptions (the obvious propaganda by which the Roswell event has been sold to the public as the crash of an alien spaceship being a good example), for three purposes: (1) *to divert public attention from other activities they wish to hide;* (2) *to influence the mass mind toward a major paradigm-shift, away from religion and objective science, and toward belief in alien visitors;* and (3), *to invoke, by mass suggestion and sympathetic magic, the demons they worship.*

---

[10] *Revelations: Alien Contact and Human Deception* (NY: Ballantine Books, 1991).

The first two hypotheses were put forward by Jacques Vallee, who clearly documents, in *Messengers of Deception* and elsewhere, the existence of just such groups and individuals clustered around the UFO phenomenon. The third hypothesis is my own. It may be that early in this century when literature on mass brainwashing first began to be published, books like *Man the Puppet: The Art of Controlling Minds* by Abram Lipsky in 1925 (which would likely have been available to Hitler and Mussolini, though this particular book seems to have been written by a Jew!), and when broadcast radio and early television were for the first time making instantaneous influence over the mass mind possible, certain black magicians realized that if they could invoke demons for themselves through self-suggestion, it might be possible to invoke them on a mass level through mass suggestion. They tried it, and it worked. They are still doing it.

As an example of how such mass suggestion might work, psychiatrist John E. Mack, in his book *Abduction*, reports that one of his patients experienced an encounter with aliens soon after viewing a TV program based on Strieber's *Communion*; another recalled an abduction after reading the book itself. (I don't know enough to accuse Strieber of deliberate demonic invocation, or to exonerate him either; I only want to point out that highly-charged demonic images have a potent life of their own.) We should not conclude by this, however, that such wizards are powerful in the sense of being more capable than the rest of us of autonomous action and choice. A psychotic arsonist or serial rapist may gain a *feeling* of great power, since it seems to him as if he is able to command the attention and vigorous action of the world around him. But it takes no power to roll a boulder down hill, or write a bad check; all it takes is an obsession that you can't control. True spiritual and social power is creative; it labors to build, to refine, to enlighten. But to ignite an entire forest with a single match is only the appearance of power; in reality it is nothing but deficiency of feeling, lack of intelligence, and weakness of will.

To employ the metaphor of addiction, we can compare a true believer's or cynical manipulator's fascination with UFOs and psychic entities to the affects of alcohol or methamphetamine on the human system. Alcohol can produce a surge of emotional energy, amphetamines a similar explosion of physical and mental energy—but the reason we experience this energy is not because it is *coming* to us, but because it is *leaving* us. It's exactly the same in the case of those who invoke entities who are fundamentally less real—in the spiritual not the material sense—than human beings: the fascination we feel for them is not something they are giving *us*; it is something we are giving *them*, something they are *stealing* from us. If today's "alien" shows many similarities to the traditional "vampire," it is because both of them steal our "blood," our life-energy, which in the most fundamental sense is nothing other than the spiritual attention we owe to God as the source of our life. As the adulterous affair destroys marriage by diverting erotic energy, so the "alien" and the "entity" destroy our relationship to God by diverting spiritual energy.

UFOs are "apports." Among the powers attributed to magicians and mediums has always been the ability to materialize objects. Such apports, however, tend to be unstable. They seem to exhibit all the characteristics of ordinary matter, yet they will often dematerialize again after a certain period. (Paramhamsa Yogananda's *Autobiography of a Yogi* is full of stories like this.) UFO phenomena exhibit the same property: undeniably real in a physical sense, they are also fleeting, as if the amount of energy required to maintain them on the material plane were too great to let them stay here for long; they are like fish out of water. And this is precisely in line with the folklore of the Jinn from all nations: they can affect the physical plane, but they can't exist here in any stable way.

To hazard a wild speculation, I can let myself wonder whether our computer technology, which has always seemed to me partly inspired by the Jinn, may represent an attempt on their part to construct bodies for themselves that *are* stable in this world, particularly in view of the fact that the Jinn and the UFO aliens seem able to interact with electromagnetic energy: automobile engines die in close proximity to flying saucers, "Raudive voices" appear spontaneously on magnetic tape, etc. If so, it would also mean that—as in the de Maupassant story "Le Horla"—they want to supplant us. But if they are so bent upon fascinating us poor, weak mortals with their superior powers, why do they apparently envy our ability to occupy physical bodies? Could it be that they know full well that the Human Form is God's image and vicegerent on earth—even if we ourselves have forgotten this—and are therefore doing all in their power to replace it, largely by tempting us to psychically and genetically deconstruct it? But if they, with all their "wild talents," apparently want to be human, just as they seem to want to make us ever more

Jinn-like, to turn us into "changelings," what does this imply about their evaluation of their own state? Perhaps they simply want to get out of the Fire.

The "aliens" do not require interaction with occultists and black magicians to appear in this world; but such alliances do make it *easier* for them, as well as providing them with conscious or unconscious agents willing and/or available to do their bidding. And the ability of these magicians to invoke alien entities on a mass level is simply one aspect of the quality of the time. According to René Guénon in *The Reign of Quantity and the Signs of the Times,*

> Since all effective action necessarily presupposes agents, anti-traditional action is like all other kinds of action, so that it cannot be a sort of spontaneous or "fortuitous" production. . . . The fact that it has conformed to the specific character of the cyclic period in which it has been working explains why it was possible and why it was successful, but is not enough to explain the manner of its realization, nor to indicate the various measures put into operation to arrive at its result.[11]

Not All the Jinn Are Evil

Not all the Jinn are demons. According to Islamic doctrine, for example, some of the Jinn are "Muslim" and some are not; the same distinction between benevolent and demonic entities can be found in Celtic fairy lore. The *Dakinis* of Tibetan Buddhism, for example—subtle entities in female form who help Tibetan yogis to attain

---

[11] *The Reign of Quantity and the Signs of the Times* (Hillsdale, NY: Sophia Perennis, 2004), 191.

Liberation—travel in a manner similar to UFOs, and are portrayed as entirely benign and helpful. In the story from the *Jetsün Kahbum* of the death of the famous Tibetan saint Milarepa,

> The *Dakinis* conveyed the *Chaitya* [the reliquary containing the saint's cremated remains] through the skies and held it directly above the chief disciples, so that it sent down its rays of light on the head of each of them. . . . And in the sky there appeared [the Tantric Deities] Gaypa-Dorje, Demchog, Sang-du, and Dorje-Pa-mo, surrounded by innumerable hosts, who, after circumambulating the Chief Deity, merged in him. Finally, the whole conclave resolved itself into an orb of light, and this sped away toward the East. The *Chaitya* . . . was transported eastward, amid a peal of celestial music. . . .[12]

Hindu *puranas* also mention travel in the subtle realm, on vehicles called *vimanas*; and such travel is not limited to demonic beings. Furthermore, the elemental spirits who form the connection between the natural world and its Creator are not evil, though they may be dangerous; the subtle, conscious archetype of a beautiful oak tree, for example, cannot be called a demon. (A friend of mine, incidentally, once saw—without benefit of psychedelics— a huge, brilliant green disc moving through the forest, passing through tree-trunks as if they were made of air: an elf-ship, apparently.)

But the Jinn who are staging the present UFO manifestations almost certainly are demons. According to Seraphim Rose, they are here to prepare us for the religion of

---

[12] *Tibet's Great Yogi, Milarepa: A Biography from the Tibetan,* ed. W.Y. Evans-Wentz (London: Oxford University Press, 1969), 300–1.

the Antichrist.[13] I agree—and I would add that anyone who wants to encounter psychic entities—good, evil or neutral—*because God isn't real enough to him* will become the demons' plaything. It may even be true, though I can't prove it, that those in the Neo-Pagan world who are attracted to the worship of elementals and nature spirits instead of the Divine Spirit may actually be seducing and corrupting those spirits, even if, to begin with, they are basically benign, or neutral. If you were being worshipped by thousands of devotees because they were fascinated by you and believed that their contact with you could give them magical powers, wouldn't you be seriously tempted? Wouldn't you be influenced to forget that your only duty is to remember God and obey His will?[14] The nature spirits are also duty-bound to remember and obey the Source of All Life; insofar as they do so, they become conduits that allow the Divine energy of the Holy Spirit to flow into and sustain the natural world. But if they forget that

---

[13] A story was posted on the web a few years ago about UFO sightings over Chechnya; apparently a flight of saucers buzzed some of the Russian aircraft attacking the Chechen rebels. One of the rebels was quoted as saying: "We don't know if they are angels or jinn, but they're on our side"—to which I would answer: "They are definitely jinn, not angels—and their goal is to get *you* on *their* side."

[14] According to *surah* 72 of the Qur'an, known as "The Jinn," verse 6: *And indeed (O Muhammad), individuals of humankind used to invoke the protection of individuals of the Jinn, so that they increased them in revolt (against Allah).* From the translation by Mohammed Marmaduke Pickthall, *The Meaning of the Glorious Koran* (New York and Scarborough, Ontario: New American Library, 1953). The translation of Mufti Taqi Usmani takes this verse to mean that their *human worshippers* increased in *Jinn* in revolt.

duty in their desire to fascinate and dominate their human worshippers, that flow of vital energy may be cut off.

So it may be true that to worship the natural world, instead of contemplating God by means of it, is actually destructive to it, that an egotistical fascination for the nature spirits may in fact be the subtle-plane archetype of the destruction of the natural world by human greed and technology.

Time-Travel and Reincarnation Related and Debunked

Those who see the UFO phenomenon as announcing a new and all-embracing paradigm, whether "religious" or "scientific," commonly associate it with the contemporary "science fiction" myths of time-travel and multi-dimensional space, which are in turn derived from imaginative speculation on Einsteinian and post-Einsteinian physics. In order to thoroughly deconstruct this paradigm I will need to take the reader on a tour through Traditional Metaphysics.

Travel in time, higher-dimensional spaces and the "multiverse" are in some ways replacing the world-view of the revealed religions, since they seem to transcend materialism and provide the "miraculous" possibilities always associated with religious faith and spiritual experience. For God all things are possible: but if all things, or many strange things, are possible to UFOs, and will be possible to human science in the future, who needs God? If space, time, matter, and even some mental processes can be manipulated by various subtle material energies, who needs grace? If time-travel is possible, who needs eternity?

This is what is believed and sometimes openly declared by those who worship elemental energies via the cult of arcane science. But in reality the myth of time-travel, based for the most part on the belief that it might be possible to locally reverse the flow of time and travel "backward," actually represents the death of the myth of progress. Here is evidence that if all coherent belief-systems are being deconstructed by post-modernism, not even scientism is immune to the process.

No less a speculative adventurer than Stephen Hawking admitted his belief that time-travel is possible. But there are irreducible logical contradictions inherent in it, or at least in our usual way of conceiving of it. We imagine that it may be possible to travel in many directions in time instead of only one, just as we can travel in many directions in space. But if time travel will become possible in the future, then—by implication—it has already happened. And if it has already happened, where are all the travelers from the future, all the historians, the archaeologists, and the tourists? They are concealing themselves, we say, because their open appearance would be too shocking for us, and would alter future history. But if they are traveling from "then" to "now," haven't they already altered future history, whether they appear openly or not? And if future history has already been altered by their time-travel, it was "always" altered. And if it was "always" altered, no "alteration" has in fact taken place...

But others maintain that they *have* shown themselves, that the "aliens" now appearing are really travelers to "now" from our own future time. Why have they come back? Perhaps for the very purpose of altering history, of saving the human race from self-destruction. But if they fail in this attempt, there will be no future human history for them to have traveled back from; and if they are destined to succeed, they have already succeeded—so they never had to make the trip in the first place. They, and we, can relax.

Some try to solve the paradox of time-travel by claiming it is possible to travel to an alternate or probable past, though not to the past we remember. But to "travel" to a "parallel" universe is not the same thing as to travel to one's own past. It may or may not be possible to separate, via arcane technology, the human body from it's own proper situation in time. But what then? That body would enter the chaos of all probable space-times, with no way to "home in" on any one of them, since its only way of "tuning itself" to a particular space-time would be based on its entire structure, which is proper to only one region or quality of space-time.

We and our lives are not two separate things—a truth that postmodern culture is doing all in its power to make us forget. Whether one is a yuppie who has thrown his or her home away to pursue the life of an itinerant globalist, or a refugee who is driven from his home by the forces of that same globalism, the post-modern human being is led to experience his or her ego as a self-enclosed monad with no organic relationship to its surroundings. And as we shift surroundings with evermore frequency and emotional randomness, we begin to believe we can shift identities in the same way, that we can be whoever we "play at" being, on a given day, or in a given moment. And so our identity either dissolves into a schizophrenic Robin Williams-like repertoire of "postures" or "routines," or else shrinks into a hard little kernel of impersonal, generic selfhood we believe can be inserted indifferently into *any* situation because no situation is really native to it. Because our psyches are chaotic and fragmented, time-travel begins to seem possible to us, even natural, because we no longer experience our own *lives* as an integral part of our own *selves.*

If we are going to apply the metaphor of travel in space to travel in time, we will have to be thorough about it. And if we are, we will be forced to admit that if it is impossible to travel in space from San Francisco to New York if there is no New York there to go to, then it would be equally impossible for me to travel from now back to the Middle Ages unless there were a "me" there in the Middle Ages for me to be.

But perhaps there was, we say. Perhaps I did lead a past life in the Middle Ages, and maybe I can travel back to it somehow. Here we can see how speculation on the possibility of time-travel makes it necessary, at some point, to posit the theory of reincarnation. If post-Einsteinian physics becomes our religion, belief in reincarnation must at some point become a dogma of that religion. Now, if I succeed in traveling back to the Middle Ages *physically*, there must already exist, in potential, a record of the fact that I did so, that the "me back then" appeared out of nowhere, or that a "second me" appeared and encountered the "me back then." But if I were to discover this record, and later decide *not* to travel back in time, where did the record come from? Where else but from a future time when I changed my mind and decided to go after all? This means that if I know there is a "me" back there for me to go to, I cannot decide not to go to him. And another way of saying "I cannot decide not to go to him" is to say "I *am* him." And if I am him, the concept of "travel" becomes meaningless. On the other hand, obviously I am not him. I am myself. This self here and now cannot be superimposed on that self there and then, because all selves, all forms, all moments, are unique, and are in fact the manifestation in the relative world of the Absolute Uniqueness of God. And so to ask if time-travel is physically possible is not like asking "is it possible for me to travel from Spain to Germany?"; it is much more like asking "is it possible for Spain itself to travel to Germany?" Who we are physically is inseparable from the time in which we live, because different times have different intrinsic qualities. According to Guénon, in *The Reign of Quantity*:

> It is evident that periods of time are qualitatively differentiated by the events unfolded within them . . . the situation of a body in space can vary through the occurrence of movement, whereas that of an event in time is rigidly determined and strictly "unique," so that the essential nature of events seems to be much more rigidly tied to time than that of bodies is to space.[15]

If I exist in a different time, I must exist in a different state. My state as a newborn infant is inseparable from the year 1948; my state as a 48-year-old man is inseparable from the year 1997, and so forth. The only way I can "travel" to 1127 is for me to assume one of the states—that is, one of the individuals—available in 1127. So at the very least, time-travel cannot be physical.

---

[15] *The Reign of Quantity*, 40.

But can it be psychic? Can it be reincarnational? Can a former incarnation of myself know me, by clairvoyant anticipation? Can I know him, by clairvoyant memory? Can we communicate with each other across the seas of multi-dimensional time?

Yes and no. That person in the Middle Ages is not me, nor am I him. As Guénon says in *The Spiritist Fallacy*,

> two identical things are inconceivable, because if they are really identical, they are not two things but one and the same thing; Leibniz is quite right on this point.

Still, we may have an eternal affinity for one another, because we are members of the same "spiritual family," emanations from the same spiritual archetype or Name of God. This does not mean, however, that information—and, by implication, causality—can travel back through time from me to him. In reality, I simply inherit certain psychic "material" from him, just as I would inherit the possessions of a deceased relative: psychic traits, unsolved problems, even memories. This is what is called "metempsychosis," which is *not* the same thing as reincarnation.

When inherited memories appear in my life, which can happen at any time from my birth until my death, it will necessarily seem to me as if I have, at least in a limited sense, gone back in time, since I am reliving another's past experiences. But in reality, those experiences have come forward in time to meet me, on the basis of an affinity—not an identity—between that past human being and myself, an affinity that is in essence eternal, not temporal. And he may also intuit my reality on the basis of the same eternal affinity, although in this case metempsychosis, or psychic inheritance, does not operate; if it did, memories of "future" lifetimes would be just as common as memories of "past" ones. He and I may discover our inner affinity over the course of our lives, by a seemingly temporal process—I by memory, he by anticipation—but the affinity itself is eternal in the mind of God; it exists beyond the plane of being where time, multi-dimensional or otherwise, has any meaning.

So the only possible conclusion is that the myth of time-travel, as well as the doctrine of reincarnation as a horizontal travel by the identical individual soul through time from one physical body to the next, is based on an inability to conceive of the real nature of eternity. Therefore, those who become obsessed with these myths are making themselves available to satanic forces whose goal is to hide from us the reality of eternity by means of a counterfeit, to so dazzle us with multi-dimensional spaces and multidirectional time-travel that we lose the ability to contemplatively imagine how God can see all things, past, present and future, as well as all probable realities, in an eternal present moment, as the "Second Person of the Blessed Trinity," the total and integral form of His Self-manifestation—in essence, not other than Himself—which, when refracted through the space-time matrix, we perceive by means of our physical senses, and name "the universe."

The Traditionalists, at least Ananda Coomaraswamy, René Guénon, and Whitall Perry, deny the doctrine of reincarnation, and claim that, while it is accepted as true by many Hindus, and something resembling it by virtually all Buddhists, it is not orthodox teaching. They explain apparent references to chains of reincarnational existences as a misunderstanding, or misapplication, of the two distinct doctrines of *metempsychosis*—the teaching that psychic as well as physical material released by the dead (including memories) can be inherited by the living—and *transmigration*—the teaching that the eternal individuality passes through many states of existence by traveling vertically (or, to be strictly accurate, in an ascending or descending spiral) on the Great Chain of Being, never passing twice through any state, including our incarnate human one. According to Guénon in *The Spiritist Fallacy*,

> transmigration . . . is a question of the passage of the being to other states of existence, states that are defined . . . by entirely different conditions than those to which the human individual is subject. . . . That is what all the traditional doctrines of the East teach . . . the true doctrine of transmigration, understood according to the sense given it by pure metaphysics, that permits the refutation of the idea of reincarnation in an absolute and decisive manner. . . .[16]

The Traditionalists maintain that not even Hinduism originally taught the doctrine of reincarnation as it is presently understood. Whitall Perry writes:

> the soul engaged in the *pitri-yana* ("Path of the ancestors") does not "coast horizontally" through an indeterminate series of lives and death[s], once having been "launched" into the *samsara*, but rather is "referred back" at the conclusion of each life to its Source; there is a vertical dimension (symbolized in the Upanishads as a return to the "Sphere of the Moon"—equatable with *Hiranyagarbha*) which means a direct confrontation (but not yet

---

[16] *The Spiritist Fallacy*, 178–79.

identity) with its primeval point of Origin. Each "life" can therefore be regarded as *original*, as a *fresh* entrance into existence or "descent," whether into a splendid or a terrible domain, and as a unique cyclic experience with a return culminating in a *theophany* or "Judgement," at which moment every soul does precisely—and with devastating clarity—recall its "former life." All the while the door of Liberation into the *deva-yana* ("Path of the gods") remains accessible to the "Knowers of Truth," once the correct responses are given that allow passage out of the *samsara* and union with supra-formal states of being.[17]

In other words, I am not a "reincarnation" of that man in the Middle Ages; in reality, both of us are unique "incarnations," or facets, of the same eternal Archetype or "Name of God."

Some uncertainty remains as to whether "soul" in the above passage refers to the unique human individuality or to the common Archetype of a whole "family" of such individualities, but this is no more than a reflection of the primal ambiguity, or rather paradox, of the traditional Hindu doctrine of transmigration: that Brahman, the Absolute Itself, is "the one and only Transmigrant"—a statement that is paradoxical because the Absolute, being beyond all relativity, is in another sense the only Reality that could not possibly transmigrate. This paradox is solved by the doctrine of *maya*: that *samsara*, though undeniably real from the point of view of the relative beings who experience it, is *illusion* from the point of view of the Absolute. God knows *samsara* as having no separate reality in itself; He sees it not

---

[17] "Reincarnation: New Flesh on Old Bones" (*Studies in Comparative Religion*, vol. 13, nos. 3 and 4, 153).

as the joys and sorrows, the struggles and choices, of num-
berless sentient beings—though He knows full well that
those sentient beings actually experience it in this way, and
knows this even more deeply than they do themselves—but
rather as the infinite Self-manifesting radiance of Himself
Alone. In other words, when I fully realize the truth that
"God is the one and only transmigrant," transmigration
ends. Furthermore, it is also known—because God knows
it—that in Reality it never began.

The failure to realize that transmigration never began
because "the one and only Transmigrant" is the Absolute
produces the ambiguous experience of transmigration,
which, as a mode of *maya*, is "both real and unreal." The
failure to understand that each transmigrational existence
is a fresh creation—as in the Islamic concept of "occasion-
alism" (the doctrine that God re-creates the entire universe
and the human soul in each new instant)—produces the
belief in reincarnation; vertical, and sovereign, Divine Act
becomes horizontal, and contingent, cause-and-effect.

The belief in reincarnation of the identical human individuality in a series of different lifetimes—a doctrine, incidentally, not taught by the Buddhists since they do not
posit a unique human individuality in the first place—sev-
ers the human soul from its transcendent Source, except at
the first origin and ultimate end of every indeterminate
"chain of lifetimes." It results in a mechanistic and deistic
universe where God can have no merciful, enlightening,
forgiving, and redeeming relationship with the worlds and
the souls He has created—a universe where, because there
can be no *dharma*, no saving Divine intervention, no religious dispensations, *karma* is absolute.

I can neither repent, in such a universe, nor can God forgive. It was this absolutization of *karma* that led Mme Blavatsky (who did accept reincarnation in her final work, *The Secret Doctrine*, despite denials by some of her followers) to hate and reject the Christian doctrine of the forgiveness of sins as a violation of the law of *karma*, and even to define prayer and sacrifice, conceived of as attempts to alter or circumvent *karma*, as acts of black magic. But to take *karma* as an absolute is absurd and self-contradictory. *Karma*, as the chain of causal actions and reactions in the relative world of *samsara*, is relative in essence; it can never be absolute. Every condition of causal inevitability on the horizontal plane can be compensated for by the operation of human freedom, and Divine Mercy, on the vertical one.

The doctrine of reincarnation is organically related to the belief in the possibility of time-travel. The mind of materialism, bound to space and time, confronts Eternity, but can neither realize nor understand it; materialism can only see "another mode of existence" as "another occasion of *material* existence." The mind incapable of transcending time can conceive of such transcendence only as a greatly-enhanced ability to travel backwards, or laterally, across indefinite horizontal dimensions, to other material realities. The sense of what Sufis call the *waqt*, the eternal Divine Presence as manifest in this particular moment, threatens that mind's most fundamental assumptions, and thus its very existence. In flight from this Presence, it takes refuge in multidimensional spaces and parallel times and reincarnational chains-of-lifetimes. Such complex, arcane theories appeal to us because, quite simply, we are afraid to encounter God. We are reluctant to admit that this unique moment is eternally saved or eternally lost according to the present quality of our love, wisdom, and vigilance, or, conversely, our hatred, delusion, and mental chaos. We want a second chance, or an infinite number of second chances, to be who we are in the sight of God. But if we are in flight from our integral identity *sub specie aeternitatis,* then all those second chances, all those future lifetimes or trips back to the past to clean up our act, are only so many new chances to go to Hell.

Time is the Mercy of Eternity, said Blake. It is given to us as a precious gift, as part of our God-given human freedom. If we waste it, there is no second chance. The *desire* to travel in time in order to escape or alter the consequences of our actions is identical with the desire not to be here now, not to be who we really are, not to pay our karmic debts by no longer trying to escape our creditors, not to sit in the Spirit and allow our debts to be forgiven by God's Mercy, not to stand in the presence of God. It is, therefore, purely satanic. To sit in contemplation is to release the past to God and receive from Him the future; to "travel in time" is to reject what God wants to give us and grab after what He wants to take away from us. In the words of the Sufi Shaykh Ibn Abbad of Ronda, "The fool is one who strives to procure at each instant some result that Allah has not willed."

Now it is true that, on the psychic plane, we already exist in a more multi-dimensional space-time than we do on the physical plane. If this were not so, visions of past and future realities, or of various "parallel" realities, would not be possible, as clearly they are. But we can't "travel" through these realities without transcending the perceptual framework necessary for physical reality, which includes linear, uni-directional time; and to transcend time is to transcend "travel" itself, and enter simultaneity.

To claim that we can transcend time in order to improve it, that we can travel to the past in order to create a better future, is like claiming we can improve conditions inside our prison cell by being released from it. But who would assert that the best use of freedom, or even a possible use of it, is to ameliorate bondage? Who else but a deluded magician, who believes he can tap a higher level of being to reinforce the agendas of a lower one, that he can use Truth to manipulate his illusions, Desirelessness to fulfill his desires, Detachment to enhance his personal power? If we consciously realize that aspect of us which transcends the space-time limits of physical reality, then the whole field of physical space-time becomes virtually available to us. But it does not become available to that part of us which is still limited to space-time. The material level of our being which, while we live, is always there, and which always retains the potential to regain control of our total perceptual field, if we let it—the part which is always saying "I'm afraid of getting old, I'm afraid of dying, I'm afraid of the end of the world, I've got to get out of here, I don't want to realize my limits, I don't want to face my end, why can't somebody freeze me so I can be revived in the future? Why can't somebody invent time-travel so I can get away into the past?"—that part of us cannot manipulate trans-material, multidimensional realities. It can never come into contact with them because, precisely, it is in flight from them. The only way for it to contact them would be for it to die to itself, and *that is the very thing it is attempting to establish contact with them in order to prevent.* This is the vicious circle of materialism attempting to access and control the Spirit for materialistic purposes, the contradiction inherent in the magical worldview, the self-defeating idolatry of subtle material forces and dimensions masquerading as the God-given freedom of the Spirit.

The Jinn do not transcend space and time, but rather exist in a different *quality* of space and time than we do in our day-to-day material lives. How this more multidimensional relation to the space-time matrix allows them to praise God in unique ways may never be known to us. But it is clear that those Jinn who are "not Muslim" realize that if they can fascinate and/or terrify us with their own multidimensional reality, which we can never fully make our own in this life, this will powerfully distract us from our own proper relationship with space-time, and thus from the unique and specifically human responsibilities God has provided us with as ways to know Him: to be born; to grow "in wisdom and age and grace"; in adulthood to struggle with the limitations of incarnate existence to protect and carry on life; in old age to acquire wisdom; at death, to meet our Maker.

Whoever doesn't want to play by these rules no longer wants to be a human being; in the words of a 1975 speech, recorded by Jacques Vallee in *Messengers of Deception*, by a member of the Heaven's Gate Cult (or Human Individual Metamorphosis, as it was then called), "a lot of people are tired of playing the human game." But the human game and the human form are the only way we can relate to the

Divine Source of our lives; all the powers of the Jinn can't change this simple fact. But they can hide it from us, and that's exactly what they are presently trying to do. It is true that, on the psychic level of our being, we are every bit as multidimensional as the Jinn are. But it is also true that we are here in physical life for a *purpose*, that we are *designed* by God for physical experience as well as for psychic knowledge and spiritual understanding, and that the purpose of physical life and uni-directional time is to continually present us with an eternal choice: to escape from the present moment, and so enter what the East Indian religions call "Samsara" and the Abrahamic ones "Hell," or to stand fully within it, and so ascend, by the vertical path that lifts us out of passing time, to "Heaven," to higher states of reality. Whether the present activity of the Jinn to distract us from this ultimate human choice is better understood as subversion from their side or an abdication of the human mandate from ours need not concern us. But the eternal choice confronting us in this present moment *must* concern us. Understanding this choice is the "one thing needful."

Religion has no other purpose but to remind us of this. Everything else is "the outer darkness, where there will be weeping and gnashing of teeth." It is nothing but a distraction—perhaps a fatal one. In *Messengers of Deception*, Jacques Vallee quotes a member of a UFO cult called The Order of Melchizedek as telling him, "we must emphasize the fact that we are receiving a new program! *We do not have to go through the old programming of Armageddon.*" But Armageddon is precisely the ultimate battle between truth and falsehood, conceived of as confronting the

entire human race at the same crucial moment. To avoid
this battle—which the forces of evil would love to make us
believe is somehow possible—is not to "transcend truth
and falsehood" (as if to make an equal mix of reality and
illusion were a sign of "balance" and "objectivity"), but
simply to embrace falsehood, and so find ourselves, in the
words of the Qur'an, "among the losers."

The attempt to circumvent God's judgement, to prevent
the consequences of human action in this world from
being fully confronted and penetrated by Divine Truth, is
a central agenda of the New Age. Unfortunately, however,
to think we can avoid the battle of Armageddon is to end
up on the losing side.

UFO Worship as Counter-Initiation

The interest in the figure of *Melchizedek* in the world of
UFO cults, which is documented by Vallee in *Messengers of
Deception*, is highly significant. Melchizedek had no father
or mother, so he is, in a sense, immortal: unborn, thus
never to die. This would place him in the same category as
the "immortal prophets" Enoch, Elias, and the Sufi Khidr,
who is often identified with Elias. (As Melchizedek was
Abraham's master in the Old Testament, so Khidr or Khezr
is the name given by Sufis to the master encountered by
Moses in the Qur'an.) According to Guénon in his book
The King of the World, Melchizedek represents the Primordial Tradition, humanity's original and perennial knowledge of eternal Truth, the trunk of that tree whose
branches are the major historical religions. *Enoch* is also big
in the UFO world, since he—like Elias, and like the
Prophet Muhammad, upon whom be peace—traveled to

57

the next world without undergoing physical death. Such "ascension" is a gift of God to a rare handful of his saints and prophets; UFO cultists, however, like to identify it with their own demonic "abductions." Contactee Jim Hurtak, for example, was given a text by his alien teachers which he published as *The Keys of Enoch*. UFO believers also regularly reinterpret Elias' "fiery chariot" as a UFO.

In *The Reign of Quantity*, René Guénon spoke of the "Counter-Initiation"—the attempt by demonic forces to subvert not only revealed religion, but also the more esoteric spiritualities, such as the Kabbalah within Judaism, Sufism within Islam, or Hesychasm within Orthodox Christianity—all of which, in their legitimate forms, are strictly traditional and orthodox, despite the heterodox distortions produced by people like Gurdjieff and Dion Fortune. In my opinion, the UFO phenomenon represents the most concentrated and wide-spread manifestation of this Counter-Initiation yet to appear, and the one most successful on a mass level.

In Whitall Perry's *A Treasury of Traditional Wisdom*, we find the following clue to the interest of UFO cultists in Enoch, provided by thirteenth-century German mystic Mechthild of Magdeburg:

> *It pleased Anti-Christ*
> *To discover all the wisdom*
> *Enoch had learned from God,*
> *So that Anti-Christ could openly declare it*
> *Along with his own false teaching:*
> *For if only he could draw Enoch to himself*
> *All the world and great honor would be his.*

According to the Traditionalist doctrine of The Transcendent Unity of Religions, all true revealed religions are renditions of the one Primordial Tradition, which is as old as humankind. This Tradition, however, cannot be accessed directly, but must be approached through one of the major world religions—otherwise one will probably encounter one of the many attempts at a kind of "generic" metaphysics, drawing upon fragments of many traditions—some system representing itself as universal but remaining cut off from the Wisdom and Grace of God, the only power that can make either a sage or a saint.

Although Truth is One, and the esoteric or mystical centers of all true religions do point directly to this same Divine Truth, "primordialism" cannot be a viable form in itself; the nourishing fruit grows on the branches of the tree, not the trunk. And, as the human door to Divine Reality, the Primordial Tradition can only be fully realized in the mystery of the soul's union with God. It would seem, therefore, that the prevalence of the figure of Melchizedek in UFO and Spiritualist lore is evidence of a satanic perversion of the Transcendent Unity of Religions.

If the doctrine of the Unity of Truth can be falsely used to deny the providential efficaciousness of the particular Divine revelations God has given, in order to promote a "New Age" religious syncretism—as is in fact happening before our very eyes—then great damage will be done to the sacred forms the Divine has established as paths for our return to the One who created us. And if the wide ways back to God are blocked (a blockage which, in God's mercy, can never be absolute), then the Powers of the Air, the nations of the *kafir* (unbelieving) Jinn, will have carte blanche to misrepresent the subtle, psychic plane as the Kingdom of Heaven, to replace wisdom with clairvoyance and sanctity with magical and psychic powers in the mind of the masses.

Again, Melchizedek had no father or mother. As such, he symbolizes the primordial Unity of Being, ontologically prior to the pairs-of-opposites that determine manifest existence. The satanic counterfeit of this transcendence-of-polarity, however, is the denial of polarity. Primordial Humanity, before the fall into time and space, was androgynous, as was Adam before Eve was separated. But the satanic counterfeit of the androgyne, as William Blake pointed out, is what he called the hermaphrodite. In Blake's system, Satan is an hermaphrodite in whom all possible states are chaotically mixed together: a perfect counterfeit of the Unity of Being, where all possibilities are embraced and synthesized by That which transcends them. Now, what falls below polarity apes what transcends it. The figure of Melchizedek, as misinterpreted by the UFO-worshippers, is thus a satanic counterfeit of principial Unity, symbolizing, among other things, the destruction of sexuality, which modern genetics has now made possible. The self-castration of the members of the Heaven's Gate UFO cult was an act of satanic worship: to destroy sexuality is to separate humanity from its archetype, and end its vicegerency.

Religion, Evolution, & UFOs

Jacques Vallee, in his book *Dimensions*[18]—possibly under the baneful influence of Whitley Strieber—speaks of the UFO phenomenon, inexplicable and numinous, as the likely origin of past, and maybe even future, religions. But in making this claim he exhibits what I can only call a shocking though very common lack of any sense of proportion, since he places in the same category demonic obsession, appearances of fairies, UFO encounters, and the apparition of the Virgin Mary at Fatima! This is like saying that whoever or whatever emerges from the same hotel—a saint, a swarm of flies, an automobile, a guide-dog, a drug-dealer or a can of garbage—must be of the same nature or have the same agenda. He is so mesmerized by the elementary fact, commonly accepted until quite recently by the vast majority of the human race, that measurable physical manifestations can emerge from the unseen, that the *quality* of what emerges entirely escapes him, largely because the *mechanism* of the emergence cannot be explained in present scientific terms—as if the divine miracles which are Christian or Muslim or Buddhist civilizations, lasting for centuries and millennia and representing the pinnacles of the human spirit, each one overflowing with exquisite art, profound philosophy, noble and dignified social mores, courageous heroism, and self-sacrifice, and which continue to produce those mirrors of God in human form—our enlightened saints— could have been thrown together by a few spooks doing

---

[18] *Dimensions: A Casebook of Alien Contact* (Chicago: Contemporary Books, 1988).

aerial acrobatics, abducting and brutalizing innocent bystanders, and raping a few women! I have the greatest respect for Dr Vallee as an objective, scientific and largely unprejudiced investigator of the UFO phenomenon, one who is at no pains to conceal his frequent horror and disgust at some of its manifestations; in *Confrontations*,[19] for example, he has a chapter on the mysterious illnesses and deaths often associated with UFO contact. He seems to feel, however, that for purposes of "objectivity" he must be careful not to draw any conclusions from this disgust. But if one's normal disgust at rotten meat represents the "organic wisdom" of the body, which is telling us that if we eat rotten meat we will get sick, then why can't he credit his emotional disgust at the UFO phenomenon as representing a similar wisdom of a psychic or spiritual order? It is here that the limits of Vallee's scientific outlook, or rather his scientific ideology, his *scientism*, make themselves apparent. Because, according to the ideology of scientism—Guénon's "Reign of Quantity"—it is not permitted to ask qualitative questions, or to base one's conclusions on qualitative considerations, *including morality*. To the degree that Dr Vallee is a good humanist, and therefore possesses a conscience and a sense of honor inherited from Christendom (though not credited to it), he is a man of culture. But one can only lament the complete lack of culture, and even of simple humanity, exhibited by those individuals (and that part of Dr Vallee) who can see and investigate nothing beyond the mechanism of

---

[19] *Confrontations: A Scientist's Search for Alien Contact* (New York: Ballantine Books, 1988).

things. Such a person must reduce an exalted religious doctrine and the incomparable civilization produced by it to a "cultural overlay" on a basically material phenomenon. Moses saw a volcano and founded Judaism; the disciples of Jesus saw a UFO and built Christendom.

But to someone with the slightest understanding of what a *religion* is, the vulgar and tasteless tricks produced by today's "aliens," whose spiritual level seems in many cases to be little above that of the neighborhood child molester, when compared with those profoundly wise, good, and beautiful manifestations which are the world's religions and wisdom traditions—as awesome in aspect as they are sublime in conception—will necessarily appear as just so much excrement. And just because a piece of excrement is pulled like a rabbit out of a hat doesn't make it smell any sweeter. It is often said that "there is no accounting for taste." I disagree. A sound taste must be based on some appreciation of the true, the good, and the beautiful, which are in the end nothing but the manifestation of God in this world, of which He alone is the Source. A degenerate taste, on the other hand, bespeaks a wounded soul—either traumatized, and so in need of healing, or deliberately depraved, and so headed for the wrath of God. I only pray that my own decision to write on the subject of UFOs does not indicate the beginnings of a similar depravity in me.

Nonetheless, Dr Vallee has done us a service in pointing out that many of the psycho-physical phenomena surrounding the appearance of the Virgin at Fatima are also commonly reported as part of UFO encounters: a perceived lowering of temperature, temporary paralysis, sweet fragrances, musical sounds, rainbow lights, the ambiguous aerial phenomenon known as "angel hair" or "the rain of flowers" (the last four being common features of apparitions of *devas* or *dakinis* in Vajrayana Buddhism), the descent of the object—in the case of Fatima, the sun—with a swinging motion, etc. Such similarities have led him to conclude that UFO manifestations and apparitions of the Virgin, or even the miracles and virgin birth of Jesus—since unexplained asexual pregnancies (which are in all likelihood demonic deceptions) are apparently sometimes reported in relation to "alien" contacts, at least according to Vallee in *Dimensions*—represent the same order of phenomena. But anyone who expects a world-wide spiritual and cultural renewal such as that brought by Jesus of Nazareth to come from "Rosemary's Baby" is deeply deluded. And the truth is, our actual expectations relating to such phenomena are often far from hopeful, whether or not we have the courage to admit it. Somewhere in our souls we all know the difference between the Son of God and the offspring of a demonic *incubus*; our horror movies, if nothing else, prove it.

As for the psycho-physical phenomena surrounding apparitions both angelic and demonic, these are best understood as simple material or quasi-material reactions to the passage of a manifestation—*any* manifestation—from the psychic to the physical plane, past the energy-border called by some the "etheric wall," which, when viewed from the material standpoint, seems in some way related to the electromagnetic spectrum, if we don't simply define it as the space-time matrix itself.

It might be permissible in this context, at least provisionally, to redefine the classical "four elements"—which are traditionally seen as the home of the subtle "elemental spirits," the gnomes, undines, sylphs, and salamanders, as: *matter* (Earth, that which stabilizes physical manifestation); *energy* (Water, that which reveals waves in motion); *space* (Air, that which represents the subtle environment of all living beings); and *time* (Fire, that which germinates, transforms, and ultimately consumes, all things). Be that as it may, the truth is that we cannot fully evaluate a veridical apparition, in terms of either its original source or its ultimate consequences, simply by cataloguing the immediate psycho-physical reverberations of its breakthrough into our world. Such manifestations may be miracles, by which I mean that they have their source in the world of spirit; they may be magical phenomena, having their source on the psychic plane alone; and, if magical, they may be either benign or demonic. In the words of Schuon, "so far as miracles are concerned, their causes surpass the psychic plane, though their effects come by way of it"[20]—which means that all apparitions, though they may come from different points of origin, must enter our world through the same door; if this were not true, "the discernment of spirits" would not be one of God's gifts, nor would Jesus have had to remind us that "by their fruits you shall know them."

Dr Vallee's scientism appears in the concluding chapter of *Dimensions*. The Introduction is written by Whitley Strieber; Vallee echoes him (unless Strieber is actually echoing Vallee) when, on page 291, he states that: "They

[20] *Light on the Ancient Worlds*, 104.

[the UFO aliens] are . . . part of the control system for human evolution." It is sad to realize that a dedicated researcher who values objectivity above all, and has consequently been able to question the dominant myth that UFOs are spaceships, and to credit not only their inexplicable physical reality but also their undeniable psychic effects and the hard evidence for human deception surrounding them, without using one truth to hide the others, completely loses that admirable objectivity when it comes to the great idol of scientism, *evolution*.

I will not here recount the many discrepancies and contradictions in Darwin's doctrine, and in other variations of the belief, which an increasing number of scientists from many fields see as rendering the theory untenable, nor will I quote from the works of those Traditionalist metaphysicians, such as Frithjof Schuon, Martin Lings, Seyyed Hossein Nasr, and Huston Smith, who explain why such a conclusion is philosophically necessary. I will only ask Dr Vallee what the abductions, the weird medical experiments, the animal and human mutilations (which he reports in *Messengers of Deception*), the aerial acrobatics designed to awe and confuse, the sexual molestations, and the use of subtle forces, either psychic or psycho-technological, which paralyze the body and darken the mind, have to do with *evolution*? If we accept the theory of biological evolution, do we not understand it as based on physical processes that have no need of UFOs to help them along? And if we are talking about social or spiritual evolution, what do terror, violation, and deception have to do with it? Can a monkey be forced to evolve into a man by torturing or hypnotizing him? Can a society be improved by confusing and terrorizing it? Can a man be forced to evolve into an angel by abducting and sexually molesting him? There is no "material proof" that the UFO phenomenon represents a conflict between Divine and infra-psychic forces for the attention of the human mind and the allegiance of the human soul, a conflict which may well be the very one named "Armageddon" in the book of the *Apocalypse*—nor will such proof ever be forthcoming. But I will submit that, to anyone surveying the phenomenon with the full range of his or her human faculties, the "unseen warfare" hypothesis must appear an infinitely better explanation than the "evolutionary" one.

Mind Control and Roswell: The Spielberg Agenda?

The deception and mind-control activities that cluster around the UFO phenomenon are discernible not only in staged manifestations of seemingly extraterrestrial landings or supernatural events, but also in certain media productions, particularly motion pictures like *Close Encounters of the Third Kind.* Anyone really interested in this hypothesis should take a look at *Close Encounters,* the *Star Wars* trilogy (1977; 1980; 1983), *ET, A Fire in the Sky* (1993), and *Roswell. A Fire in the Sky,* the story of a supposedly true-life alien abduction, is a fairly innocent, straightforward account of a intensely traumatic event. *Star Wars,* though not without sinister elements common to all science fiction, is an old time "space opera." The moral it draws may be opposed at many points to traditional spiritual doctrine, but still, for all its use of mythological themes provided by "mythic advisor" Joseph Campbell, it is essentially an adventure story told for purposes of entertainment, and not deliberate propaganda. *ET* is extremely suspect, particularly since it features a parody of Michelangelo's image in the Sistine Chapel of God creating Adam by touching his finger. It regularly produced a kind of maudlin, pseudo-religious reaction in people to whom all normal religious emotions were apparently foreign, but there is nothing in it that can't be explained by the generally-accepted anti-clericalism and aesthetic satanism endemic to Hollywood culture.

Close Encounters of the Third Kind, on the other hand, with its exaltation of the psychopathic tendency prevalent in contemporary culture to cut all one's economic and emotional ties in the pursuit of some fantastic and empty ideal, is another matter; from the time it first came out, I have always thought of it as a mind-control job. It is nothing less than a satanic counterfeit of the "rapture": instead of sound doctrine and religious faith, in the context of the intense psychic and spiritual energies unleashed at the apocalyptic end of the aeon, leading to the ecstatic experience of the presence of God, it presents emotional nihilism, spiritual emptiness, and the lack of any stable frame of reference as the prerequisites for a willing capitulation to inhuman forces—and presents this outcome as "positive." The "hero" of the movie throws his entire life away to pursue the source of the sound in his head of a few musical notes and the mental image of a barren desert crag—experiences which various forms of hypnosis and mind-control may well be able to produce with the greatest of ease—and is rewarded by being willingly abducted by an alien spaceship.

That many who viewed *Close Encounters* took it as much more than mere entertainment was demonstrated to me in the late '80s, when I attended a party at the house of New Age musician Constance Demby. A few notes of music had appeared mysteriously on one of her audio tapes! Our blithe and enthusiastic hostess played them for us, and interpreted them, not surprisingly, as a personal message from the Space Brothers, on the model of the musical notes in *Close Encounters*. It goes without saying that no one in the room contradicted her; one of the most effective methods of self-induced mind-control, as we all know, is based on fear of the social *faux-pas!* [NOTE: Not being a film buff, it was only after I finished writing this chapter that I realized the three productions that seemed most like mind-control to me—*Close Encounters, ET,* and *Roswell*—were all produced by Steven Spielberg! No one, of course, should draw any hard conclusions from this; it may be that Mr Spielberg simply has a mind-control-like style of motion picture production.]

The 1994 TV "docu-drama" *Roswell,* starring Martin Sheen, about the supposed crash of an alien spaceship in New Mexico in 1947, and the recovery both of alien corpses and surviving aliens who later died, will serve as an even better example. Jacques Vallee, in *Revelations*, tells us why he believes it unlikely that the Roswell incident was the crash of an alien spacecraft. He also gives us an interesting piece of information that contradicts the TV version of the event. According to Vallee, the first people who (according to *Roswell*) reached the supposed crash site encountered another group already there, who described themselves as "archaeologists." Vallee speculates that their real role may have been to plant the mysterious material later claimed to be debris of the spaceship—material which, according to him, could easily have been produced by human technology as it existed in 1947. In *Roswell*, however, the statement is made that the object could not have been a crashed experimental aircraft because "they'd be looking for it" if it were, but no one appeared; the site, when first approached after the incident, was deserted. Obviously these two accounts do not add up.

Among the more common mind-control techniques, useful to anyone who cares to implement it, and that can command sufficient attention via the media or the internet, is the Government Coverup Ploy: if you assert that a given fact is true, but that the government is covering it up, a certain percentage of the public will automatically believe you—especially if you can pressure the government to the point where it will start issuing denials. It's a cheap and reliable tool; even the government itself can use it. *Roswell* is based upon the Government Coverup Ploy, as are a number of even more obviously propagandistic "documentaries" and "leaks" relating to the Roswell incident that have subsequently appeared. But *Roswell* is also a good specimen of two much more sophisticated mind-control techniques, ones that must be classed as satanic, since they represent perversions of specific metaphysical principles. I have named these techniques *subliminal contradiction* and *deferred closure*. [NOTE, 2021: *The document entitled "The Art of Deception: Training for a New Generation of Online Covert Operations," lifted by Edward Snowden from the NSA website in 2014* (https://theintercept.com/document/2014/02/24/art-deception-training-new-generation-online-covert-operations/)—*it's made up of the images from a Power-Point presentation minus the text of the lecture—contains a grid of 20 mind-control techniques called "Gambits for Deception." Subliminal contradiction and deferred closure, since they are designed to produce a state of cognitive dissonance, would fall under the gambit known as "Create Cognitive Stress" (column 1, row 4). Interestingly enough, three of the images from "The Art of Deception" are photographs of UFOs!]*

In the words of Jacques Vallee,

> It is possible to make large sections of any population believe in the existence of supernatural races, in the possibility of flying machines, in the plurality of inhabited worlds, by exposing them to a few carefully engineered scenes, the details of which are adapted to the culture and superstitions of a particular time and place.[21]

Fr Seraphim Rose comments:

> An important clue to the meaning of these "engineered scenes" may be seen in the observation often made by careful observers of UFO phenomena, especially CE-III [*close encounters of the third kind, i.e., sightings of sentient aliens*] and "contactee" cases: that they are profoundly "absurd," or contain at least as much absurdity as reality. Individual "Close Encounters" have absurd details, like the four pancakes given by a UFO occupant to a Wisconsin chicken farmer in 1961; more significantly, the encounters themselves are strangely pointless, without clear purpose or meaning. A Pennsylvania psychiatrist has suggested that the absurdity present in almost all UFO cases is actually a *hypnotic technique*. "When the person is disturbed by the absurd or the contradictory, and their mind is searching for meaning, they are extremely open to

---

[21] *Passport to Magonia: From Folklore to Flying Saucers* (Chicago: Henry Regnery Co., 1969), 150–1.

thought transference, to receiving psychic healing, etc.
([Vallee] *The Invisible College* [E. P. Dutton], 115).[22]

Precisely. In the technique of subliminal contradiction, two mutually incompatible bits of information are simultaneously projected into the perception of the victim without the contradiction being either pointed out or explained. In the technique of deferred closure, inexplicable data are continually fed to the victim or victims over a period of time, data that always suggest the possibility of a rational explanation but never quite allow it. And since the human mind is designed to seek and produce both perceptual and rational closure, the mind subjected to deferred closure will react to the continued frustration of one of its most basic needs either by sinking into stunned exhaustion, or by producing a paranoid, delusional form of closure. Schizophrenia presents the mind with a flood of data that overwhelms the normal processes of emotional, rational, and perceptual closure; paranoid schizophrenia represents a more or less successful attempt to reach relative closure by abnormal means. Deferred closure, then, might be defined as an experimental method for producing paranoid schizophrenia.[23]

Subliminal contradiction and deferred closure are not only mind-control techniques, however; they are essential elements of postmodern "philosophy," which believes that contradictory statements are not necessarily mutually

---

[22] *Orthodoxy and the Religion of the Future*, 130.

[23] For a fictional description of this technique, see C. S. Lewis, *That Hideous Strength: A Modern Fairy-tale for Grown-ups* (New York: Macmillan, 1968).

exclusive, and that any closure as to the true nature of things, any "overarching paradigm," is impossible. Postmodernism, both as a philosophy and as a name for our contemporary culture, employs subliminal contradiction and deferred closure simply because it can't imagine anything else; it no longer believes in the existence of objective truth. (This, in itself, is enough to explain "the Spielberg Agenda," although not to absolutely disprove the existence of a more deliberate attempt at "social engineering.")

In *Messengers of Deception* we are introduced to UFO contactee Rael (Claude Vorilhon, whose patronymic subsequently appeared on the TV sci-fi series *Babylon 5* as the name of an alien race, the Vorilhons), a robed and bearded false prophet who wears a medallion based on a design supposedly shown him by the aliens. The design—a combination between a swastika and a star of David—is an instance of subliminal contradiction. And since the contradiction is addressed to the "right brain" in the form of an image, rather than to the "left brain" in the form of a statement, it is more likely to be accepted uncritically, since the role of the right cerebral hemisphere is to synthesize data, not analyze it. As soon as a subliminal contradiction is accepted into the field of perception without initial resistance, the critical faculty is stunned, and the mind becomes receptive to suggestion.

I wonder if anyone besides myself has seen the subliminal contradiction ploy as it operates in normal social situations. If a person who wishes to influence you can establish a clear image in your mind of who he is and what is to be expected of him, and then, swiftly and nonchalantly, say or do something that totally contradicts this image without exhibiting the normal mischievousness or social anxiety such a shift usually entails, you may accept both your image of him and its contrary simultaneously, and subliminally. If you do, he has stunned you into a state where you can easily be manipulated. A subliminal contradiction between speech and body language can have the same effect.

The UFO phenomenon as a whole, and the crop-circle phenomenon as well, is a case of the deferred closure technique. Are UFOs spaceships? Psychic entities? Human deceptions? Are they wise philosophers come to aid us, or sinister invaders here to destroy us? The ambiguity of the phenomenon in itself produces a state of deferred closure, but it is clear from Dr Vallee's researches that this ambiguity is also being deliberately exploited by human groups. If you put a person in a prison cell along with a sledgehammer, a Barbie Doll, a can of olives, and a ball of copper wire, and tell him you'll let him out again as soon as he invents a philosophical system based on these four "principles," he may astound you with his ability to make "closure" on the intrinsic meanings of and inter-relationships between elements which, in any objective sense, do not allow for it. His "system" will say much more about his own deepest hopes, fears, beliefs, and root assumptions than it will about the data you've provided him. And once you know what his "system" is, you can stress him further by feeding him data that again contradict it, ruining his meticulously-constructed pattern. Even better, you can feed him data that triumphantly confirm it—and onto which are grafted other items of information you want him to accept as implicitly true. And he *will* accept them, because he experiences them not as alien beliefs being forced upon him against his will, but as parts of a pattern *he himself has created* through his own labor, imagination, sacrifice, and quest for truth.

Roswell is filled with subliminal contradictions, and the entire plot is an example of deferred closure. It is the story of Jesse Marcel, an Air Force officer who visits the crash site and picks up some of the mysterious material of which the craft was supposedly constructed—and later, in the course of a government coverup of the incident, is forced to lie about his experience. Jesse is the archetypal misunderstood paranoid crank, with whom many Americans can identify—but *we* the omniscient observers know he's telling the truth. We see him years later at a reunion of his old outfit, dying of emphysema. He's still determined to expose the coverup and get to the bottom of what really happened. He runs into a few others who had something to do with the incident, and hears the story about the recovery of alien bodies, and one live occupant. As the stories are told, we see flashbacks to 1947, some supposedly authentic, some only dramatizations of rumors. There is no resolution. Finally the mysterious UFO researcher and/or government agent and/or anti-government agent, Townsend (the Martin Sheen character) approaches Jesse and tells him more about the bizarre intricacies of the UFO phenomenon than he ever knew—referring, in the process, to *Close Encounters of the Third Kind*, the one other UFO film, except possibly *ET,* I picked out as a mind-control experiment—but leaves him as oppressed and puzzled as ever. Townsend has no final conclusions either, but nonetheless remains mysteriously knowledgeable and intimidating; after meeting with him, Jesse sinks into despair.

Whenever the incident is described in the movie, contradictory accounts are given. The alien bodies are smooth-skinned/no, their skin is scaly; their heads are egg-shaped/no, they are pear-shaped; the crashed object is flat and crescent-shaped (we see a quick flash of it)/no, it is egg-shaped (we see a quick contradictory flash); the name of the mortician who was contacted by the Air Force is Paul Davis/no, David Paulus. The bodies number five or six/no, three or four; the bodies are human-like/no, child-like (as though children aren't human)/no, foetus-like; the ship is cylindrical/no, round/no, egg-shaped/no, dome-shaped: the disorienting patter goes on and on.

At one point we are shown a newspaper headline from the *Roswell Daily Record* reporting on the official debunking of the incident as a crashed weather balloon: *"Gen. Ramey Empties Roswell Saucer."* This, on the face of it, means little or nothing, unless it is a bad pun on the act of pouring out spilled tea. Subliminally, it means two different and contradictory things: That the general "empties" the incident of meaning—i.e., calls it unreal—and that he *unloads* the saucer itself, indicating that it is a real object out of which real things can be taken, presumably the alien bodies. Since this is apparently an actual headline of the time, we can't attribute the subliminal contradiction it contains to Steven Spielberg. So how can we explain it?

Elaborate conspiracy theories aside—such as the involvement of the intelligence community in all aspects of the Roswell incident from day one—perhaps someone on the staff of the *Roswell Daily Record* who believed in the crash constructed the headline so as to debunk the official debunkers. Or it may simply represent—and this in no way invalidates the above explanations—the intuitive reaction of the human mind, on a deeply unconscious level, to "archetypal idea" of the UFO as a "messenger of deception."

The action is repeatedly intercut with religious imagery. When Jesse first shows the mysterious saucer-material to his family, it appears below a picture of Jesus on the wall of his home. When Townsend makes his mysterious and mystifying revelations to Jesse, the scene begins with a priest giving a memorial service for deceased fliers outside a hangar; Townsend takes Jesse inside the hangar, tells him the UFO secrets, then leaves. At the end, we return to the memorial service and the priest. The scene is designed to give the distinct though subliminal impression that the Catholic service is the outer or exoteric form, *and the UFO-lore the inner or esoteric meaning.*

The themes of the sacred *temenos*, temple, or mystery-cave, and the initiatory experience as a spiritual death (the memorial service) are also exploited—but not a death and *rebirth*, since Jesse remains inside the hanger and never re-emerges, in that scene, into the sunlight. The suggestion is that the UFO phenomenon is equivalent to, and will in due course replace, revealed religion—a suggestion made more explicit in the scene where the Air Force brass assigned to investigate the incident repeat the belief that "aliens" have manipulated human genetics and inspired human religious leaders throughout history, and are told by their superior, "Think of our religious institutions if all of this were to just come out, what are people going to believe in?" and the scene where Jesse's son tells his dying father, who believes he's close to discovering the truth, "You're close to nothing. Face it, Dad, you're never going to find what you're looking for, you just want an answer like there's some proof out there of God, or an afterlife, UFOs, it's all the same thing, something to hang on to when nothing makes sense, this is fantasy, to make you feel better in the night." So in the face of death, that "nothing," that "night," no faith is permitted; knock, and no door will be opened to you.

But the real goal of *Roswell* and other UFO-related propaganda is revealed in the scene where an officer participating in the investigation is shown in a picture gallery, looking up (briefly, so as to set up a "waking suggestion") at a portrait of a haloed saint (apparently based on a portrait of St. Augustine by the 17th-century painter Philippe de Champaigne) who is gazing upward and to his right at a light-beam suggestive of God's glory—or a beam from a UFO—but holding in his left hand a red object emitting white flames, flames that are actually kindling his halo; the object appears to be the head of a demon. The officer is asking: "Under what agency will we be operating?" His colleague answers him, "None, we will have complete control." Here we can begin to see the meaning of the tradition that Satan has saints and contemplatives of his own, who answer to neither God nor man. On the other hand, the saint is *under* the light-beam in the painting, just as the officer is under the painting itself; word and image and directly contradictory on a subliminal level. And the fact that the saint holds the demon's fiery head—if that's what it is—in his hand (in de Champaigne's painting it is a flaming heart), shows that he is in control of it, or believes he is, much as the ceremonial magician of the Renaissance would invoke the power of God, or one of His angels, to give him control over the demon he wished to enslave. Here the desire for Promethean spiritual autonomy is used to deny the truth that the sorcerer, even though he clearly worships his own self-will as if it were God, is in fact handing that will over to the control of an infernal will by that very worship. This is the "denial'—and also the "co-dependency"—that affects all magicians: self-determination is enslavement, but every worshipper of self-determination must deny this, until it is too late.

Roswell also does what it can to muddle and neutralize the findings of honest researchers like Vallee. When the military big-wigs are discussing how to cover up the Roswell crash, one asks "what if people think we are not in control of the skies?" and another answers "they'd be right"—thus setting up another subliminal contradiction to "we're in complete control." Then they propose that "hoaxes" be carried out, and that true information be leaked through unreliable and suspect sources as part of the coverup. But why hoaxes? How can a convincingly staged UFO appearance or landing convince people that there are no such things as UFOs? It can do so only if it is later proved to be a hoax—but that is the one thing almost never absolutely provable when UFO deceptions are alleged. All that Vallee has been able to come up with are tantalizing clues that a particular manifestation could have been a deception, and evidence convincing enough to suggest that the phenomenon as a whole includes deception activities by human groups.

But if anything is clear in this murky world, it is that whatever deceptions are being carried on are meant to be believed, not to be disproved. As for leaking of true information via untrustworthy sources, that *is* being done, in order to set up a "feedback loop" between the lunatic cranks and the cynical debunkers. But the purpose of such a loop, according to Vallee in *Messengers of Deception*, is to discourage objective investigation of the phenomenon, *not* to convince people there are no such things as UFOs. If that were its purpose, one would have to conclude that it is not a very effective strategy, given that every time someone who has investigated the actual data, or has himself experienced the phenomenon, hears it cynically debunked by the "authorities," academic or military, those authorities lose more credibility in his eyes—and every time that person or someone like him voices his or her legitimate feeling that the authorities are either deluded or dishonest in regard to the phenomenon, the officials in question become even more cynical and self-defensive, and so lose that much more *authority* over those upon whose trust they depend. And into that vacuum of social and cultural authority come—the UFOs.

Jacques Vallee believes that this method of discouraging objective investigation is largely for the purpose of hiding the activities of human groups, possibly allowing them to test new high-tech weapons, or "psychotronic" devices for the manipulation of human consciousness, without public or political interference. I agree. But there are other reasons for it. This lowering of collective consciousness and diminishment of our sense of reality is being deliberately engineered for two purposes: first, in order to make the public more suggestive and open to a belief in UFOs, and secondly to lull us into a false sense of "security"—really a psychic numbness based on repressed fear—so that we will not realize that UFOs represent a mass psychic invasion of the most alarming nature, requiring an immediate and militant response on the plane of spiritual warfare.

This *abaissement de niveau mental* is served by a number of devices, not the least of which is the tendency to portray aliens in comic mode, which completes the triad of Fear/ Worship/Complacency that can be seen around other horrendous possibilities—that of human cloning, for example. We fear them; we laugh at them in order to deny our fear; as soon as our fear is suppressed, we accept them. This engineered unreality is symbolized in *Roswell* by the alcoholic haze in which the stories of the UFO crash are exchanged at the Air Force reunion; one of the informants, sluggish and overweight, appears floating on his back in a swimming pool with a drink on his belly. It's not an image designed to promote either critical awareness or spiritual vigilance.

The central intent of the writers and producers of *Roswell* surfaces in the scene where Townsend is "educating" Jesse Marcel in the hangar; the following is an excerpt from their dialogue:

> Townsend: One must proceed cautiously here, on guard against one's desire to want it to be true or want it not to be true. One must be, as much as possible, neutral.
>
> Jesse Marcel: Well, how can you be neutral? A thing is either true or it's not, there is no middle ground.
>
> T: Alright, alright . . . then none of it is true.

J: *None* of it?

T: Well, maybe some of it…

J: No, no, you're playing with me—why are you playing with me?

T: Because maybe you wouldn't even know what was true if you'd seen it all for yourself. How's that for an answer?

J: Alright, then what did I see out there in that field?

T: That? . . . why, that was a weather balloon.

J: *No*, it wasn't, I know what I saw, and it was not from this world.

T: Don't you understand, Jesse, you have *nothing*, just a lot of old memories and second-hand recollections. Nobody is going to take you seriously, not without proof, not without hard evidence.

What is being preached here is nothing less than the impossibility of arriving at objective truth, and ultimately the unreality of objective truth itself. Irreducible subjectivities, with no overarching paradigm to unite them into an integrated vision of reality, are all we have—all we are. It is the whole postmodern age and postmodernist agenda in a nutshell; and since objective Truth is ultimately God, what is being preached is also a denial of God, and His replacement by demonic principalities and powers. But without grounding in the Divine objectivity of the Ground of Being, even our ability to draw rational conclusions from empirical data becomes eroded, since rationality is nothing less than a distant mental echo of Intellection, or Divine Gnosis. In the words of C.S. Lewis from *That Hideous Strength* (1946), his science fiction novel about an invasion of earth by the forces of the Antichrist (which I heard Traditionalist author James Cutsinger describe as "*The Reign of Quantity* in fictional form"):

> The physical sciences, good and innocent in themselves, had already . . . begun to be warped, had been subtly maneuvered in a certain direction. Despair of objective truth had been increasingly insinuated into the scientists; indifference to it, and a concentration upon mere power, had been the result. Babble about the *élan vital* and flirtations with panpsychism were bidding fair to restore the *Anima Mundi* of the magicians. . . . The very experiences of the dissecting room and the pathological laboratory were breeding a conviction that a stifling of all deep-set repugnances was the first essential for progress.

The heart of the matter—which appears in the first two passages of the above dialogue—is a *deliberate* and *engineered* attack upon the concept of objective truth; the postmodernist deconstructionism of academia is nothing but the stifling vapor rising up from a much deeper and darker cauldron. When Townsend says we must be on guard against *wanting* the extraterrestrial hypothesis to be true or not true, he is accurately presenting one of the prerequisites for real objectivity—then, instead of the word "objective," he uses the word *neutral*. But neutrality is not necessarily objectivity; it can just as easily denote nihilism or indifference. And Jesse senses this nihilism, which is what leads him to reject the stance of neutrality, to protest that "A thing is either true or it's not, there's no middle ground." But as Townsend has set things up, Jesse defeats himself by this very protest, since *he has been manoeuvred into defending objectivity by attacking the very criteria of objectivity*, which have falsely been associated with a nihilistic neutrality—a neutrality which, in this context, is really nothing but another name for "suggestibility."

[NOTE, 2021: *The postmodern denial of objective truth, however, will inevitably produce a longing for certainty. When this longing becomes sufficiently desperate, particularly on the part of people with little or no ability to determine what is objectively true because they are addicted to subjective impressions, the day will come when they will be willing to accept any ideology that gives them a feeling of certainty and closure, no matter how absurd or outrageous. This is how a late postmodern liberalism, where granting the "equal right to be heard" to any worldview from the sublime to the ridiculous had assumed dogmatic status, was able to produce an inquisitorial movement like Cancel Culture which claims the absolute authority to suppress all opposing views. And it is not beyond the realm of possibility that the social engineers thoroughly understand this principle and have learned how to use it to alter collective belief.*]

How ingenious, how cunning, the writers and producer (Steven Spielberg) of *Roswell* were, and are. But if they're so smart, one is led to ask, why can't they be intelligent? Because that would not be in the interest of the forces they consciously or unconsciously serve; all intelligence is of God.

A truly inverted and satanic *metaphysics* is at the root of *Roswell*. Subliminal contradiction is a satanic counterfeit of the metaphysical principle that the Absolute is beyond the "symplegades," the pairs-of-opposites. Deferred closure is a satanic counterfeit of the metaphysical principle that the Infinite cannot, by definition, be contained within any system of thought or perception. Absoluteness and Infinity, according to the metaphysics of Frithjof Schuon, are properly descriptive of the Divine Essence of God, and nothing else. To apply them to anything relative and contingent, anything in the realm of cosmic manifestation, is the highest form of idolatry, perhaps best characterized as a deception of "Iblis," the Muslim name for Satan, or the satanic principle, in its most metaphysically subtle mode of action.

The Absolute, or Necessary Being, is not realized by an amalgamation or confusion of the pairs of opposites, but by transcendence of them, after which it is seen exactly how the Absolute manifests by means of them. And the Infinite, or Possible Being, is not realized by a foredoomed attempt to reduce the Infinite Possibility within the Divine Nature to a closed system, but simply by accepting what comes and letting go of what must go, in the knowledge that all things are a manifestation of God's will, either in terms of what He positively wills—Being, or the good—and what He negatively allows—the privation of Being, or evil—given that the universe, though it manifests Him, is not He Himself, and is thus necessarily imperfect. Submission to God's will as manifest in the events of our lives—a submission that does not exclude, but actually requires, our creative response to these events, since our innate desire to live shapely and fully-realized lives is also part of God's will—leads to the gnosis of all events as acts of God, which opens in turn on the deeper gnosis of all manifest forms as derived from eternal, archetypal possibilities within the embrace of the Divine Infinity. The realization of God as Infinite is not the desire for an ultimate philosophical or experiential closure, but the sacrifice of this desire in the face of the Divine Immanence; the realization of God as Absolute is not the horizontal confusion or neutralization of polarities, but the vertical intuition of their common Principle in the light of the Divine Transcendence.

In the last scene, we see Jesse Marcel hopelessly puttering around the crash site in the dry autumn grass, looking for "hard evidence"—remnants of the UFO crash debris which were all collected thirty years ago. He is seeking for certainty not where it can really be found, in the objective Ground of Being, but precisely where it can never be found: in memory. Jesse, his wife, and his son come together again as a family around a sense of a bleak, nostalgic futility: "We can never know the truth," the movie says, "but at least we can huddle together emotionally on the basis of a common despair of knowing it."

And so *Roswell* ends with one more satanic counterfeit: that of *humility*. Instead of a pious awe in the face of what transcends form, we are left with a stunned, mesmerized hopelessness in the face of what has never reached it, or has fallen below it. Nonetheless, as Rumi says, counterfeit coins only exist because there really is such a thing as true gold; or, in the words of Meister Eckhart, "The more he blasphemes, the more he praises God." So the spiritual practice, here, is not to struggle with the shadows of contradiction and uncertainty, but to turn 180 degrees away from them. It is to let the counterfeit remind you of the True: to make hopeless contradiction a way of remembering the Absolute Divine Truth that eternally possesses the power to resolve it, and endless uncertainty a way of remembering the Infinite Divine Life that radiates from the core of that Truth, by which we can, in Blake's famous words,

> *see the world in a grain of sand*
> *And Heaven in a wild flower*
> *. . . hold Infinity in the palm of your hand*
> *And Eternity in an hour.*

False humility before what is less real than you are makes you arrogant, and destroys your human dignity. True humility before what is infinitely greater than you are blesses and uplifts you, which is why Muslims say that man, *because* he is God's slave, is thereby His vicegerent, His fully-empowered representative in this world.

Abduction: The Ontological Agenda

Alien contact represents an irruption into the material plane of subhuman forces from the subtle realm, whose goal is the dissolution of our world. But though dissolution is the natural end of any cycle of manifestation, we aren't required to capitulate to the forces that produce it, because there is a spark of the Divine Nature within us which is beyond manifestation entirely, which was not veiled by its beginning nor corrupted by its fall, and will not be altered by its end. But if we forget this, if we turn our spiritual attention away from the Spirit of God and toward the forces of chaos and subversion that are It's shadow, then our return to Him—which, according to the Qur'an, is the destiny of all beings—will be indefinitely delayed, and will ultimately take place by the dark road of infernal torment, not the road of God's Mercy, the path of Divine Love and Wisdom.

The Alien Disclosure Deception

According to René Guénon, as you will remember, the adoption of materialistic beliefs by the mass of mankind is inseparable from an actual "solidification of the world." But materialism has already moved past its apex, a truth Guénon saw in 1945, and that is much more obvious today. In the late nineteenth century, when materialist ideology was at its strongest, both religion and "superstition" were debunked. But today, as this ideology continues to lose power, and belief in subtle beings and invisible worlds becomes more acceptable, such acceptance does not take the form of a return to religion and metaphysics, which continue to be eroded, but rather that of a collective fascination with mysterious and sinister possibilities, exactly as Guénon predicted. The post-modern "transcendence" of the modernist paradigm, to which materialism was integral—Marx and Darwin being two of modernism's central pillars—has resulted not in a renaissance of traditional theology but in a nihilistic worship of fragmentation and chaos in the name of the "celebration of diversity." Postmodernism shows itself to be a toxic stew in which arcane science, disintegrated cultural material, and "infra-psychic" forces are mixed in relatively equal amounts. In Guénon's own words:

> The materialistic conception, once it has been formed and spread abroad in one way or another, can only serve to reinforce the very "solidification" of the world that in the first place made it possible . . . the "solidification" . . . can never be complete, and there are limits beyond which it cannot go. . . . [The] farther "solidification" goes the more precarious it becomes, for the lowest degree is also the least stable; the ever-growing rapidity of the changes

taking place in the world today provides all-too-eloquent testimony to the truth of this. . . . [Though] the hold of materialism is slackening, there is no occasion to rejoice in the fact, for cyclical manifestation is not yet complete, and the "fissures". . . can only be produced from below; in other words, that which "interferes" with the sensible world through those "fissures" can be nothing but an inferior "cosmic psychism" in its most destructive and disorganizing forms, and it is moreover clear that influences of this kind are the only ones that are really suited for action having dissolution as its objective . . . everything that tends to favor and extend these "interferences" merely corresponds, whether consciously or otherwise, to a fresh phase of the deviation of which materialism in reality represented a less "advanced" stage. . . . In the Islamic tradition these "fissures" are those by which, at the end of the cycle, the devastating hordes of Gog and Magog will force their way in, for they are unremitting in their efforts to invade this world; these "entities" represent the inferior influences in question.[24]

No clearer presentation of the "ontological agenda" of today's "aliens" is available to us than the book entitled *Abduction: Human Encounters with Aliens*,[25] by Pulitzer Prize winning author and Harvard psychiatrist John E. Mack. Based on nearly one hundred cases of "alien abduction," Dr Mack (like Jacques Vallee, whose preeminence as a UFOlogist Mack affirms) concludes that such abductions are real, and that they are carried on by entities from subtler planes of being who have the power to physically impinge upon this one. He delves more deeply than Dr

---

[24] *The Reign of Quantity,* 145, 147, 202, 206.
[25] New York: Scribner's, 1994, 412.

Vallee into the ongoing psychological and psycho-physical "covenant" that is often established between aliens and their abductees, but ignores, for some reason, Vallee's findings about the involvement of human groups practicing deception and mind-control.

According to Mack, alien abduction seems to run in families. Many abductees had alcoholic or emotionally frigid parents, came from broken homes, or suffered childhood sexual abuse. Mack mentions one study in which the abduction experience is related to ritual abuse by satanic cults. Interaction with "aliens" can begin as early as the age of two or three. In childhood they often appear as relatively benign, but when the abductee reaches puberty their actions become more sinister. Abductees sometimes transfer to the aliens feelings of love that were not reciprocated in the family setting, and experience being loved in return. Many abductees, in Mack's estimation, seem particularly psychic or intuitive; many experience the development of psychic powers as a result of the abduction itself.

The "aliens" exhibit characteristics commonly encountered in shamanism; they, or their craft, sometimes appear as animals. They also bear an obvious resemblance to traditional "gods, spirits, angels, fairies, demons, ghouls, vampires, and sea monsters"—though it appears Mack is incapable of differentiating between the various types of subtle beings, or doesn't want to. And though UFO sightings are a world-wide occurrence, most abductions are reported from the Western hemisphere, with the United States heading the list.

(The correlation of UFO activity with emotional frigidity has an interesting sidelight: Breakaway Freudian psychoanalyst Wilhelm Reich, the father of much of today's "bodywork," was attempting toward the end of his life— when many believe he had become mentally imbalanced —to manipulate and enhance a subtle "life-energy" he named "orgone" as part of his struggle against the "emotional plague." This was his name for a *mass freezing of human emotion*, often expressed in terms of what he called "character armor," as well as through social movements such as Nazism. According to Reich, UFOs, as a source of "deadly orgone energy," were in part responsible for this plague.)

The alien abductors subject their victims to terrifying and humiliating "medical-like" procedures. They also voyeuristically view them performing sexual intercourse, or themselves have intercourse with them. One of the major agendas of the aliens seems to be to extract human sperm and egg cells from their abductees so as to genetically engineer a "hybrid" human/alien race (cf. Genesis 6:1–4). Female abductees experience these hybrid fetuses being placed in their womb, then somehow removed a few months later, to continue their growth aboard alien "spacecraft."

Their "mothers" are sometimes re-abducted, and then directed to show mother-love to these hybrid beings, who appear "listless." *No evidence exists of actual physical pregnancies.* After abduction, many victims experience themselves as now possessing, or as always having possessed, a dual "human/alien" identity; they sometimes see themselves as performing the same "procedures" or "experiments" upon new abductees as were originally performed upon them.

Among the case histories Dr Mack presents are some of

the most horrifying stories of demonic attack and possession I have ever encountered, though he does not recognize
them as such. He admits that

> Abductees . . . bear physical and psychological scars of
> their experience. These range from nightmares and anxi-
> ety to chronic nervous agitation, depression, even psycho-
> sis, to actual physical scars—puncture and incision marks,
> scrapes, burns, and sores.

He speaks of broken marriages and alienation of affection
between parents and children as among the more common after-effects, and says that negative physical and psychological effects persist even in cases where spontaneous
healing of chronic or incurable diseases occurs. One
would naturally assume, therefore, that his therapeutic
approach would include an attempt to shield his patients
from ongoing alien influence, and help them break any
psychological ties that might remain. But this is not in fact
the case, because Mack, appallingly, believes that the
influence of the aliens, by and large, is good! He views his
role as one of helping his clients to remember their abduction experiences, often via hypnosis (which, incidentally,
has been proved so unreliable as a tool for accessing
"recovered memories" that the courts have disallowed testimony based upon it)—and then helping them deal with
the violent and horrific emotions such memories entail—
*and then helping them accept that their experience is (some-
how) ultimately "positive," "transformative," or "spiritual."*
He sees himself as supporting them more against skeptical
therapists and family members than against the alien kidnappers themselves.

"In my work with abductees," he says, "I am fully

involved, experiencing and reliving with them the world that they are calling forth from their unconscious." One gets the distinct impression that the therapeutic session with Dr Mack is actually the missing second half of the abduction experience itself, which includes both an original deeply traumatic event or series of events, and the eventual acceptance of the experience, *in contradiction to all the patient's deepest feelings*, as a "message" or "mission" from the aliens, in the "permissive," "supportive," "non-threatening," "non-judgmental," "accepting" therapeutic framework provided by Dr Mack. It would be interesting, however, to see how some of Mack's patients would react in a different environment—that of a traditional exorcism, for example. Would their deliberately suppressed feelings of being profoundly violated reassert themselves in such a context? Would the full acceptance of these feelings lead to a radically different conclusion about the aliens' true agenda? Mack himself seems to view his interaction with his clients as part of the "composition" of the abduction experience. He describes it as a "co-creative" process, "the product of an intermingling of flowing-together of the consciousness of two (or more) people in the room. Something may be brought forth that was not there before in exactly the same form." Precisely.

Reading Mack is like watching, through a two-way mirror, the putterings of a confused physician who is so fascinated by the task of diagnosing a disease that he has forgotten that it is his duty to heal his patient. Perhaps he simply doesn't know how to begin to treat the disease that confronts him. But one can only conclude from his book—since he comes right out and says it—that he accepts the alien agenda reported by his tormented and traumatized patients, *because they themselves accept it.* Is this the final form of the "client-centered therapy" of Carl Rogers? The idea that, since the patient has chosen schizophrenia, or demonic possession, the role of the psychiatrist is to support him in this choice, and help him go crazy?

Of course the client "accepts" the alien program: he is possessed by it, precisely as a human cell invaded by a virus, which utilizes the cell's own genetic structure to create replicas of itself, is possessed by the virus. But just because a person's immune system fails to overcome the attack of a microbe, do we therefore second it in its "choice"? Is this good medical practice? (Not for nothing did C. S. Lewis, in *That Hideous Strength,* call the demonic space-beings and/or fallen angels battling to conquer earth the "Macrobes.")

Mack casts about for scattered fragments of spiritual and occult lore to explain what his patients are going through, and comes up with little more than evidence that such things have always occurred, coupled with speculations based upon the statements made by the aliens themselves! But if someone kidnaps and tortures me, is that any indication that I ought to believe what he says? Is such an attitude in any way rational, not to mention sound on the level of normal human emotion? And the fact that similar things have occurred throughout history is purely elementary. The power of realities from unseen dimensions to impinge on our world has always been part of human knowledge, its suppression by reductionist materialism over the past couple of centuries notwithstanding. Mack builds his case for accepting the alien agenda on the fact that their very presence overturns the materialist paradigm. But if so, then why can't he accept the common consensus of the pre-materialist millennia, when it was well understood—as it still is by many today—that manifestations such as he reports indicate the presence of demons, and that demons are, in every case where it serves their ends—and sometimes because they simply can't help themselves—deliberate liars? He gleefully profits from materialism's denial of the validity of religion and of any sense of moral order in the universe; it is precisely what allows him to accept a purely demonic reality of a subtle nature—coupled with a sinister and self-contradictory philosophy—and then introduce it as the herald of a major paradigm-shift *because it transcends materialism.* This is exactly what Guénon meant when he said that materialism first "solidifies" the human mindset, and then produces "fissures" opening not on the "celestial" but on the "infra-psychic."

The correct practice when confronted with such manifestations as alien abduction, for which the hard evidence continues to mount, is simply to admit the obvious—that such manifestations exist—and then proceed to ask the questions that will immediately occur to any normal, religiously-educated human being: (1) Is the manifestation in question good, neutral, or evil? (2) If it is good, what does it ask of us? (3) If it is neutral, is it useful or a waste of time? (4) If it is evil, how can we avoid and/or combat it? Someone who cannot ask even these most elementary and inevitable of questions is in no way a physician of souls. And, unfortunately, Mack falls into this category. He seems to believe that to ask moral questions about what appear to be the deliberate actions of conscious beings is somehow unscientific, and repeats the common nihilist cliché, derived from a counterfeit metaphysics, that beings from subtler planes are in some way beyond good and evil. He ignorantly attributes this counterfeit metaphysics to Tibetan Buddhism, and opposes it to that of Judeo-Christianity:

> To the polarizing perception of Christian dualism these dark-eyed beings seem to be the playmates of the Devil (Downing, 1990). Eastern religious traditions such as Tibetan Buddhism, which have always recognized the vast range of spirit entities in the cosmos, seem to have less difficulty accepting the actuality of the UFO abduction phenomenon than do the more dualistic monotheisms, which offer powerful resistance to acceptance.[26]

In relation to the belief that higher realities are morally neutral, Frithjof Schuon's teaching on the subject is as follows: God may be "beyond good and evil" because He transcends all relativity, but this does not mean that He is "beyond good," or morally neutral in His relation to us, or somehow half-good and half-evil. He is the Sovereign Good, beyond any conceivable relationship with the fragmentary and privative manifestation we call "evil." His goodness transcends definition as "the opposite of evil," not because it is in any way involved with evil, but because it is Absolute, and consequently has no opposite.

When Mack uses the word "acceptance" in the above passage, does he mean "acceptance as real" or "acceptance as good and/or inevitable," as when he helps his clients in

[26] New York: Scribner's, 1994, 412.

the therapeutic setting to overcome their natural resistance and *accept* the alien agenda? He seems to be saying that Tibetan Buddhism, with its understanding of "the vast range of spirit entities in the cosmos," accepts them as real, whereas the Christian tradition does not. But Christianity, in seeing the aliens as "playmates of the Devil," obviously does accept them as real, by Mack's own admission. Mack makes the word "acceptance" deliberately ambiguous in order to imply that, while Christianity narrow-mindedly rejects the aliens as evil, broad-minded Tibetan Buddhism accepts them as a natural part of the cosmos; but all he has really been able to factually assert is that the Tibetan Buddhists believe they are real—which, of course, is also true of the Christians. His obvious intent is to drive a wedge between Christianity and Buddhism, and to imply that the Tibetans, in accepting aliens as real, necessarily accept them as good, as if Tibetan Buddhism possessed no doctrine of the demonic. Such, of course, is not the case. Both Christianity and the Vajrayana recognize the existence of demonic entities, the difference being that Christians believe they are eternally damned, while Buddhists hold that after their karmic debts are paid they can move on to relatively less infernal modes of existence, and that great saints can, on occasion, even convert them to Buddhism! But their profoundly destructive effects, and the need to vigorously combat them spiritually, are fully recognized by both traditions; to imply the contrary is either culpably ignorant or effectively slanderous to Tibetan Buddhism. And just because demons are esoterically understood in the Vajrayana as apparitions conceived in one's own mind, which symbolize obscuring attachments and passions, in no way makes them less real; after all, the human form itself is also an apparition conceived in one's own mind—which is ultimately the mind of the Buddha—symbolic in this case of the "human state hard-to-attain," the only state from which the potential for Perfect Total Enlightenment can be realized.

Padmasambhava, the great Vajrayana adept who brought Buddhism to Tibet, spent a lot his time combatting and subjugating demons. The following passages are from *The Tibetan Book of the Great Liberation* by W.Y. Evans-Wentz:

> Then Padma thought: "I cannot very well spread the Doctrine and aid sentient beings until I destroy evil" . . . he subjugated all . . . demons and evil spirits, slew them, and took their hearts and blood into his mouth. Their consciousness-principles he transmuted into the syllable *Hum* and caused the *Hum* to vanish into the heaven-worlds. . . . Transforming himself into the King of the Wrathful Deities, Padma, while sitting in meditation, subjugated the Gnomes. . . . Padma performed magical dances on the surface of a boiling poisonous lake, and all the malignant and demoniacal *nagas* inhabiting the lake made submission to him . . . he subjugated various kinds of demons, such as those causing epidemics, diseases, hindrances, hail, and famine. . . . Padma brought all the gods inhabiting the heavens presided over by Brahma under his control. . . . And, in other guises, Padma conquered all the most furious and fearful evil spirits, and 21,000 devils, male and female . . . the goddesses Remati and Ekadzati appeared before Padma and praised him for thus having conquered all evils and all deities.[27]

[27] London: Oxford University Press, 1968, 139–42.

In line with Mack's findings, the aliens should obviously be classed among the "demons causing diseases and hindrances"—but if he is so respectful of Tibetan Buddhism, why doesn't he see them as forces to be subjugated? I assume it is because he is no more a Vajrayana Buddhist than he is a Christian, though he feels no shame at taking the doctrines of both traditions out of context and using them for his own ends. "There can be little place," he says, "especially within the Judeo-Christian tradition, for a variety of small but powerful homely beings who administer an odd mixture of trauma and transcendence without apparent regard for any established religious hierarchy or doctrine." [412] But, as we have just seen, Judeo-Christianity has a perfect place for them: the infernal regions. Their lack of "regard" for any "established religious hierarchy or doctrine" clearly does not represent an inability on the part of the revealed religions to make sense of them, but rather a will on the aliens' part to discredit the revealed religions—an agenda that Mack, as demonstrated in the above passage, supports. And there is no better way to undermine revealed religion than by associating the idea of "transcendence" with the idea of "traumatic violation," thus separating the True from the Good in the victims' minds, and associating Truth, not with Goodness, but with evil, and naked power (thereby also, by implication, making the Good appear weak).

According to traditional metaphysics, pure Being is in itself the Sovereign Good whom we call God; consequently the more real something is the better it is, and the better something is the more real it is. It is the goal of the Antichrist to separate Truth from Goodness and Love, and unite it instead with ruthless power, so as to wipe Goodness and Love from the face of the earth.

Mack repeatedly answers critics who attribute the abductees' acceptance of the aliens' agenda to the "Stockholm Syndrome," the documented psychological tendency of victims to identify with their tormentors, as Patty Hearst did with the terrorists who kidnapped her. He says:

> In contrast to the narrow and self-serving purposes of human abusers and political kidnappers, the beings reveal a shared purpose, and offer the possibility of opening to an inclusive, more expansive worldview that is powerfully internalized by many abductees. [339]

But Patty Hearst was also opened to a "shared purpose" based on an "inclusive, more expansive worldview"—that of global class struggle as opposed to the sheltered life of a rich and spoiled playgirl—by the Simbionese Liberation Army; and any child whose first sexual experience is with an abductor or molester has certainly had his or her worldview widened, though in a terribly destructive manner. There is no necessary contradiction between a "self-serving purpose" and a "more expansive worldview." Hitler, who was not only self-serving but made the act of serving him into a pseudo-religion, opened some extremely expansive vistas to the German people. Unfortunately for them, and for the rest of the world, they were vistas of evil.

On page 407, Dr Mack attempts to *defend humiliating and dehumanizing abuse* as a positive and transformative experience. He says:

> I am often asked how experiences that are so traumatic, and even cruel at times, can also be spiritually transformative. To me there is no inconsistency here, unless one

reserves spirituality for realms that are free of pain and struggle. Sometimes our most useful spiritual learning comes at the hands of rough teachers who have little respect for our conceits, psychological defenses, or established points of view.

Whatever his intent, such a sweeping statement might be construed as a defense, not only of the "right" of aliens to abduct us, but of the "right" of megalomaniac gurus and unethical psychiatrists *to psychologically and sexually abuse their devotees and clients.* It is true that the Nazi death-camp experience was powerfully transformative in a spiritual sense for some Jews; Elie Wiesel and Victor Frankl come immediately to mind. But does this mean that the Nazis were a spiritual force for good in the world? In the words of Jesus of Nazareth: "There needs be evil, but woe to him through whom evil comes." Whether one believes in UFOs and alien abduction or not, the grave dangers of Mack's approach should be obvious.

Incredibly, Mack sees the abduction experience as a paradigm of "personal growth and transformation." On pages 48–49 he presents it systematically in terms of eight elements, or stages.

(1) Pushing through ego-death to acceptance;

(2) Recognizing the aliens as intermediaries between the human state and an impersonal cosmic consciousness;

(3) Experiencing ecstatic return "Home" to this consciousness;

(4) Recalling past lives;

(5) Gaining an expanded consciousness which transcends the material level and includes great cycles of reincarnational manifestation;

(6) Identification of one's consciousness with a vast array of other forms of consciousness, including those of elemental spirits and dinosaurs;

(7) Experience of human/alien dual identity;

(8) Attainment of a multi-dimensional consciousness which seems to transcend the space-time matrix.

Let us deal with these items one at a time:

(1) The *falsehood* here is the identification of the willing surrender of one's ego with the forcible breaking of one's will. God is not a hypnotist or a terrorist. A deep and fertile relationship with the Source of All Life cannot be the product of brainwashing and mind-control. Therefore whatever forces employ such techniques are opposed to God. As C. S. Lewis writes in *The Screwtape Letters*, speaking through the mouth of his demon Screwtape:

> To us a human is primarily food; our aim is the absorption of its will into ours, the increase of our own area of selfhood at its expense. But the obedience which the Enemy demands of men is quite a different thing. . . . His service [is] perfect freedom. . . . We want cattle who can finally become food; He wants servants who can finally become sons.[28]

According to the Qur'an [2:256], *there is no compulsion in religion.*

(2) The Jinn are, in a sense, intermediaries between the human state and higher conscious realms, simply because they inhabit a subtler plane of the Great Chain of Being—

---

[28] New York: Macmillan, 1973, 37–38.

but to believe that they can be intermediaries *for us* is a *falsehood*: they are not on the "human stem." And if the Jinn we encounter happen to be what the Christians call "fallen angels"—subtle-plane beings who have turned against the Source of Life through a perverted use of their free will—they can only act as effective intermediaries between us and our own spiritual destruction. When Jesus said, "none come to the Father but through me," one of the things He meant was that no human being can unite with God by any other avenue than God's Humanity. As the Muslims say, human beings relate to God by virtue of our *fitrah*, our primordial, God-created human nature. Consequently, the image of God as an "impersonal cosmic consciousness" is another partial *falsehood*. On the *first* level of the Great Chain of Being, God is Beyond Being, the unknowable Divine Essence, the "Godhead" of the mystics; but we have no access to this Godhead except through the *second* level, through the personal God. And this God is not a separate Being, but is of one Essence with the Godhead. The Godhead is not impersonal, in other words, but *transpersonal*; if the Divine Personhood were not a potential within the Transpersonal Godhead, that Personhood could never appear. To believe otherwise is to identify self-transcendence and mystical Union with alienation and dehumanization. And this is an all-too-common counterfeit image of the spiritual Path in many people's minds, one which the aliens—as actual "spirits of alienation"—are here to exploit.

(3) The ecstatic experience of a return "Home"—a name for the aliens' point-of-origin that is taken directly from

the motion picture *ET,* by the way—can only, given the horrific context, be a demonic *falsehood.* Because the aliens have access to the psychic plane, they can of course produce intense psychic experiences, as Mack repeatedly demonstrates; such experiences, as we well know, can even be initiated by chemicals. And given the hangover from materialism that still afflicts us, it is easier for them than ever before to palm off psychic experiences as spiritual realizations, since hardly anyone nowadays is taught even the need for a "discernment of spirits," much less the necessary criteria, and since anything of a subtler quality than the dead material level of today's ambience will likely seem "numinous."

According to Dr Mack, most (but not all) UFO abductions appear to be "out-of-body experiences." Seraphim Rose has this to say of such experiences:

> It may be asked: What of the feelings of "peace" and "pleasantness" which seem to be almost universal in the "out-of-body" state? What of the vision of "light" which so many see? . . . These experiences are "natural" to the soul when separated from the body. . . . In this sense the "peace" and "pleasantness" of the out-of-body experience may be considered real and not a deception. Deception enters in, however, the instant one begins to interpret these "natural" feelings as something "spiritual"—as though this peace were the true peace of reconciliation with God, and the "pleasantness" were the true spiritual pleasure of heaven.[29]

[29] *The Soul After Death* (Platina, CA: St Herman of Alaska Brotherhood, 1980), 115–16.

(4/5) Once again, transcendence of gross bodily consciousness is no proof of spiritual development, or even of a valid spiritual experience. And recall of past lives, as we have already seen, is a *falsehood* if taken literally. Furthermore, since it remains on the psychic plane alone, the plane of "metempsychosis," it is in no way spiritual.

(6) The identification of one's consciousness with a vast array of other types of consciousness is a mark of psychic dissolution, not spiritual development. The human mandate is first to realize one's total dependence upon God, and ultimately to see oneself with God's eyes, thereby becoming identified with the eternal Archetype of Humanity within the Divine Nature, the "primordial Adam." Through the eyes of this Divine Humanity, we can contemplate, and gain insight into, other forms of consciousness—organic, psychic, and spiritual; this is the meaning of the story in Genesis that "Adam named the animals," and the similar story in the Qur'an that "God told Adam the names of all created things": he saw into their essential natures, the Names of God which were, and are, their eternal archetypes. But to allow one's consciousness to flow horizontally into other non-human and sub-human forms via *a departure from the human form* is called "insanity" on the psychic plane and "damnation" on the spiritual one. According to the Qur'an, after Allah created Adam, he commanded the angels to prostrate themselves to him. Every angel obeyed, except Iblis, the Muslim Satan. To open one's psyche to the endless variations of cosmic manifestation without remaining faithful to one's human form, as it exists in the mind of God, is to prostrate

oneself to Iblis, and enter "the darkness outside, where there will be weeping and gnashing of teeth."

(7) The experience of human/alien dual identity is multiple-personality disorder on the psychic plane, and demonic possession on the spiritual one. As the vampires of folklore turn their victims into vampires, so the alien kidnappers "turn their victims into aliens" by "stealing their souls"—by destroying their identification with their own humanity.

(8) The mark of true higher consciousness is Unity: "Hear, O Israel, the Lord our God, the Lord is One." The multi-dimensional kaleidoscope of the Jinn-world is destructive to Unity unless seen with the eyes of Unity: and only contemplative identification with what is higher than us on the Great Chain of Being—not with dinosaurs, who are lower than us (not to mention being extinct!), or elemental spirits, who, though subtler than us, are not *central* like we are (being something like the sparks or reverberations of the Primordial Adam on the subtle material plane)—can give us those eyes.

The aliens are liars. As Mack himself admits, "I would not say that aliens never resort to deceptions to hide their purposes." [415] And one of their lies is that the reason they deliberately suppress abductees' memories of the abduction experience is to "protect" their victims. (The real purpose, in my opinion, is to allow the seed of psychic control to mature undisturbed.) Mack, on the other hand, claims that he has seen no evidence that recall causes any harm. Shouldn't this in itself clue him in to the potential harmfulness of deception? But of course, as he admits, deception presents no problems for him, and certainly hasn't led him to question the abductors' motives. Such naivete, in any other situation, would destroy the credibility as an objective researcher of the person exhibiting it. It does so here.

Mack's desire to be deceived seems to have completely destroyed his critical faculties, which is why he can make the following absurd and contradictory statement with, presumably, a straight face:

> Through [the aliens'] interaction with the abductees they bring them (and all of us potentially) closer to our spiritual cosmic roots, return us to the divine light or "Home," a "place" (really a state of being) where secrets, jealousy, greed, and destructiveness have no purpose. The aliens, on the other hand, long to experience the intense emotionality that comes with our full embodiment. They are fascinated with our sensuality, our warmth, our capacity for eroticism, and deep parental affection, and they seem to respond to openhearted love. They act at times like love-starved children. They delight in watching humans in all sorts of acts of love, which they may even stage as they stand around watching and chattering as the abductees perform them. [415–16]

At this point it seems almost unfair to take advantage of Dr Mack's vulnerability by pointing out the dizzying inconsistencies in the above passage—but duty calls: if the aliens come from a "Home" where secrecy has no purpose, why do they so often keep their abductions secret by wiping all memory of them from the minds of their victims? If destructiveness has no purpose there, why are they so destructive, physically, socially, and psychologically, to those unfortunate enough to encounter them? If they

107

delight in our parental affection, why is alienation of affection between parents and children often one of the after-effects of abduction? And what does voyeuristically watching, if not pornographically staging, acts of human sexual intercourse have to do with love?

"The human/alien relationship itself evolves into a powerful bond," says Mack.

> Despite their resentment and terrorization, the abductees may feel deep love toward the alien beings, especially toward the leader figures, which they experience as reciprocated, despite the cold and business-like way the abductions themselves are conducted. The aliens may be perceived as true family, having protected the experiencers from human depredations, disease and loss.

But Mack, in the very same book, has documented how the aliens themselves commonly produce disease and loss! Again we are shown, with nauseating clarity, how denial is only a virtue to the true believer.

The "powerful bond" that some abductees develop with their tormenters is, of course, no proof that the relationship is healthy, because—as we all know—*evil tempts.* C.S. Lewis, in *That Hideous Strength*, provides this chillingly accurate description of the demonic temptation of his hero by forces of the Antichrist:

> Suddenly, like a thing that leaped to him across infinite distances with the speed of light, desire (salt, black, ravenous, unanswerable desire) took him by the throat. The merest hint will convey to those who have felt it the quality of the emotion which now shook him, like a dog shaking a rat; for others, no description will perhaps avail. Many writers speak of it in terms of lust: a description admirably illuminating from within, totally misleading from

without. . . . Everything else that Mark had ever felt—love, ambition, hunger, lust itself—appeared to have been mere milk and water, toys for children, not worth one throb of the nerves. The infinite attraction of this dark thing sucked all other passions into itself: the rest of the world appeared blenched, etiolated, insipid, a world of white marriages and white masses, dishes without salt, gambling for counters. . . . But it was like lust in another respect also. It is idle to point out to the perverted man the horror of his perversion: while the fierce fit is on, the horror is the very spice of his craving. It is ugliness itself that becomes, in the end, the goal of his lechery; beauty has long since grown too weak a stimulant. And so it was here. The creatures . . . breathed death on the human race and on all joy. Not despite but because of this the terrible gravitation sucked and tugged and fascinated him towards them.

Significantly, Mack finds that "Virtually every abductee receives information about the destruction of the earth's ecosystem and feels compelled to do something about it." [413] The aliens sometimes ask the abductees why they are so destructive; for some reason the abductees usually do not think to ask the same question of them. Abductees are very often shown horrendous images of future ecological devastation, and even of the actual splitting and disintegration of the globe, and emerge more "environmentally sensitive" than they were before.

The "human / alien hybridization program" is presented by the aliens as a response to the state of the environment. According to Mack,

Both men and women come to feel despite their anger [at being abducted] that they are taking part—even that they have chosen to participate—in a process that is life-creating and life-giving. Furthermore, for most abductees the hybridization has occurred simultaneously with an enlightenment imparted by the alien beings that has brought home forcibly to them the failure of the human experiment in its present form. Abduction experiencers come to feel deeply that the death of human beings and countless other species will occur on a vast scale if we continue on our present course and that some sort of new life-form must evolve if the human biological and spiritual essence is to be preserved. *They generally do not question why the maintenance of human life must take such an odd form.* [italics mine]

But of course a hybridization that appears to be happening on the subtle plane is not biological, nor is the essence of the alien/human hybrids really human, any more than that of the humanized ape produced in Italy in the 1980s, in which ape and human DNA were combined. In both cases, the result is a direct betrayal of the human essence, not its preservation. (Here we have good evidence, incidentally, that the demonic forces known as "aliens" may in fact be providing the inspiration for the science of genetic engineering, particular when it is applied to human beings. It's as if the geneticists, virtually all of whom believe man evolved from ape-like ancestors, are somehow being forced to prove, in actual practice, the doctrines of their traditionalist opponents, who assert—as does the Mayan book the *Popol Vuh*, among other ancient texts and traditions—that apes are really degenerate men.)

And the images of the earth splitting in two provided by the aliens are curious. No amount of humanly-produced environmental devastation could have this effect. Apart from being a possible image of the "cracks in the downward direction" in the "great wall" spoken of by Guénon, one logical conclusion would be that such images are being used to terrorize us to the point where we will sacrifice our sexuality, and our humanity itself, to the alien terrorists who show them to us; the self-castration of members of the Heaven's Gate cult may have the same significance. They are apparently using our legitimate fear of environmental destruction and the end of the world to confront us with a temptation that can be summarized as follows:

Nature is more important than the human form—therefore abandon your humanity, betray the human archetype which is placed directly above you in the Divine Nature, and worship instead what is below you. Do not return sexuality to its archetype in God, via normal human love and reproduction; give your erotic, emotional, and reproductive energies instead to the demonic and the infra-human. If you do this you can avoid God's judgement; you can avoid the confrontation with the Divine archetype of your Humanity, and not have to see how you have fallen away from it and betrayed it; you can avoid death, or at least species death; the human form can still live (the lie goes) *in sub-human form, as a demonic/human hybrid. If you want to avoid being sent to Hell, simply go to Hell on your own.*

They are imposing this temptation by means of the deepest and most intense of natural human emotions: life-creating sexual passion, and the fear of universal death. As any good brainwasher knows, terror is one of the two most effective tools for breaking the subject's will; *relief* is the other. And when terror is intense, sometimes sexual desire is the only refuge from it. Knowing this, the aliens produce the greatest fear of which they are capable, and then offer sexual desire as a way out. By this method they appropriate the sexuality of their victims, and gain a degree of power over them that is extremely hard to counter, since if an attempt to break free is proposed, the victim fears that the terror will return.

"The aliens stress the evolutionary aspect of the species-joining process, the repopulation of the earth subsequent to a total environmental collapse" says Mack. [417] But then what becomes of the "environmental sensitivity" the aliens reportedly produce in their victims? What good is environmental sensitivity in a dead world? And how can one love the earth, and wish to preserve it, if one's "love of the earth" is the product of abduction, terror, and violation of one's human integrity? What experience could be better designed to make us *hate* the earth, and despair of doing anything to save it? What better way to make environmentalism repellent to religious believers than to associate it in their minds with demonic activity? And what better way to subvert environmentalism itself than to set up a false opposition between humanity and nature by claiming that the only way organic life—including human life—can survive is if we abandon our humanity? If the "human experiment" has failed in its present form, if total environmental collapse is inevitable, then who's going to be motivated to preserve the natural world? And how can action to preserve the natural world be trusted to be environmentally healthy if carried on by someone with such a negative system of beliefs? Do we hire someone to reorganize our business who tells us up front that he's convinced we're going to fail? In view of this mass of deception designed to misrepresent their motives, I can only conclude that the real aim of the "aliens" is to use our fear of the end of the world, and our guilt for destroying it, as an opportunity to lure us to our damnation.

So this is the triple demonic temptation of the latter days: (1) To worship the natural world in itself rather than worshipping God by means of it; (2) To divert our sexual powers in a sub-human direction; and (3), To directly betray the human form. And the three are intimately related, since to divert our powers of reproduction and the profound human emotions that are a natural aspect of them in a non-human direction is perhaps the most effective way of betraying our humanity; and to betray our humanity is the most effective way of destroying the earth, since our abdication of the God-given responsibility to act as His vicegerent in the material world is at the basis of our worship of sub-human ideologies, including materialism; and materialism is the worldview out of which have sprung the sub-human technologies which are destroying our planet. "Where man is not, nature is barren," said William Blake—to which the aliens reply, in effect, "If dehumanization is destroying the earth, maybe *total* dehumanization can save it," while simultaneously diverting our attention, for a moment at least, from the fact that they have already told us that it *can't* be saved: subliminal contradiction in its most terminal form. Fortunately, from all indications, the alien "visitors" are not to be believed. They are not reliable teachers—to say the very least. And sometimes the aliens themselves admit this. In an account by Jacques Vallee, humanoid aliens told an abductee that they contact people by chance, that they "want to puzzle people," and ordered him "not to speak wisely about this night."[30] If Dr Mack

---

[30] *The Invisible College: What a Group of Scientists has Discovered about UFO Influences on the Human Race* (NY: Dutton, 1975), 17, 21.

had been the abductee, I'm sure he would have been only too glad to comply with this directive.

A Counterfeit Second Coming

The myth of the UFO holds great power over the contemporary mind; it is a true sign of our times. This is due to the fact that, for all its sinister implications, there is an archetypal reality behind it. To take one example, even though UFOs appear in many different shapes—Jacques Vallee in *UFO Chronicles of the Soviet Union*[31] says that Russian UFOlogists are more willing than their Western counterparts to admit that the phenomenon is "polyvalent"—the shining disk known as the "flying saucer" has exercised more influence on the popular imagination than any other. Why is this?

Carl Jung, in *Flying Saucers: A Modern Myth of Things Seen in the Sky* (1959), saw in their circular shape a symbol of his "Self Archetype," and thought that the phenomenon represented a collective longing for the Second Coming of Christ—a longing which, in my opinion, is being co-opted by the Jinn who serve Antichrist, and diverted, through collective fascination, toward a satanic counterfeit of the *parousia*.

Many UFOlogists, Erich van Däniken among them, have interpreted the vision of God's Throne in the first chapter of *Ezekiel* as a UFO manifestation, based on the brightness and swiftness of the "four living creatures"

---

[31] Jacques Vallee in collaboration with Martine Castello, *UFO Chronicles of the Soviet Union: A Cosmic Samizdat* (NY: Ballantine, 1992).

(*hayoth*) who supported the Throne, and on the association of the creatures with "wheels" and "rings full of eyes" and "a wheel within a wheel." But Ezekiel's vision was not a sensual vision of meaningless and deliberately paradoxical aerial acrobatics produced by the Jinn, but an *intellectual* vision of God's creative power manifesting in, and as, the universe. If the Throne appeared to his physical eyes, it was only because the *meaning* of the Throne had already dawned upon his heart.

Leo Schaya, in *The Universal Meaning of the Kabbalah*, provides the symbolic meaning of Ezekiel's vision, which ought to be sufficient to allow anyone with the slightest degree of spiritual intuition to see the vast difference in *level* between the UFO phenomenon and a true *theophany*:

> The "throne," in its fullness, is the first and spiritual crystallization of all creatural possibilities before they are set in motion in the midst of the cosmos. When the "throne" assumes its dynamic aspect and cosmic manifestation begins to move, it is called the divine "chariot" (*merkabah*); then the four *hayoth,* or peripheral axes of creation, spring from the "throne" become "chariot," like "lightning darting in all directions," measuring all the dimensions and all the planes of manifested existence. Under the aspect of "torches," "brilliant lights," or spiritual "flashes" of lightning, the *hayoth* are also called *kerubim* [cherubim], "those who are close" to the living God, that is to say who emanate directly from God in action. While the hayothic axes are traveling in all the directions of the cosmos, out of them come "wheels" (*ofanim*), or angelic powers, which play a part in actualizing the spherical forms and cyclical movements of the created; their spiral

vibrations—as it were "a wheel within another wheel"—are called "whirlwinds" (*galgalim*).[32]

As the Antichrist counterfeits Christ, so the UFOs counterfeit God's Throne, which in Muslim as well as Hebrew metaphysics represents the apex of the created order, and in Christian terms appears as the "Throne of the Lamb" at the center of the Heavenly Jerusalem.

The aliens are here to mimic spiritual realities on the psycho-physical level, and so prepare the way for Antichrist. As St Symeon the New Theologian says in the *Philokalia*:

> Men will not understand that the miracles of Antichrist have no good, rational purpose, no definite meaning, that they are foreign to truth, filled with lies, that they are a monstrous, malicious, meaningless play-acting, which increases in order to astonish, to reduce to perplexity and oblivion, to deceive, to seduce, to attract by the fascination of a pompous, empty, stupid effect.[33]

As our taste in art, architecture, social forms, and human relationships is jaded in these latter days, so is our taste in miracles. According to Seraphim Rose:

> Serious scientists in [the former] Soviet Union . . . speculate that Jesus Christ may have been a "cosmonaut," and that "we today may be on the threshold of a "second coming" of intelligent beings from outer space. (Sheila Ostrander and Lynn Schroeder, *Psychic Discoveries Behind the Iron Curtain*, Bantam Books, 1977, 98–99). . . . Per-

---

[32] *The Universal Meaning of the Kabbalah* (Hillsdale, NY: Sophia Perennis, 2005), 74.

[33] Quoted in *Orthodoxy and the Religion of the Future*, 145.

haps never since the beginning of the Christian era have demons appeared so openly and extensively as today. The "visitors from outer space" theory is but one of the many pretexts they are using to gain acceptance for the idea that "higher beings" are now to take charge of the destiny of mankind. . . . [The] "message" of the UFOs is: prepare for Antichrist; the "savior" of the apostate world is coming to rule it. Perhaps he himself will come in the air, in order to complete his impersonation of Christ (Matt. 24:30; Acts 1:2); perhaps only the "visitor from outer space" will land publicly in order to offer "cosmic" worship of their master; perhaps the "fire from heaven" (Rev. 13:13) will be only part of the great demonic spectacles of the last times. At any rate, the message for contemporary mankind is: expect deliverance, not from the Christian revelation and faith in an unseen God, but from vehicles in the sky.[34]

To avoid being drawn into the camp of the Antichrist, we must overcome, with God's help, the triple temptation presented above. We must *remember* that the forms of nature are not to be worshipped, but rather that we are called upon to worship the invisible and transcendent God by means of them, recognizing them as symbolic manifestations of eternal realities hidden within the Divine Nature. As St Paul says, "For the invisible things of Him from the creation of the world are clearly seen, being understood by the things that are made, even His eternal power and Godhead." [Rom. 1:20]

We must *remember* the sacredness and symbolic depth of our sexual powers and natures. In the words of James Cutsinger:

---

[34] *Orthodoxy and the Religion of the Future*, 102, 140–42.

[What C.S. Lewis calls] this "real polarity" [of gender] is to be found, not only as Lewis suggests in creatures, however superhuman, but all the way up to the Divine Reality itself ... which is the ultimate Source of everything else, and which for that reason is the source and paradigm of all distinctions. In its absoluteness and transcendence, the Divine is the archetype for everything masculine, while its infinity and capacity for immanence are displayed at every level of the feminine. ... [The] polar qualities revealed to us as sex are actually and objectively on every plane of the ontological hierarchy. ... As Seyyed Hossein Nasr has written, "The difference between the two sexes cannot be only biological and physical, because in the traditional perspective the corporeal level of existence has its principle in the subtle state, the subtle in the spiritual, and the spiritual in the Divine Being itself.[35]

Gender is in fact so integral to our humanity that the way in which we live it out, or sublimate it, or dedicate it, is one of the things that determines whether or not we remain united with our human archetype. To let our sexuality fall into the power of non-human forces is to depart from the human form. To dedicate it to a fully human love, or directly to God as in the monastic vocation, is to worship God by means of the human form.

Lastly, we must *remember* what the human form really is. Allah, in the *ahadith qudsi* (the traditions in which God Himself speaks), declares that "Heaven and earth cannot contain Me, but the heart of my believing slave can contain Me." And in the words of St Gregory of Nyssa:

[35] "Femininity, Hierarchy and God," in *Religion of the Heart*, ed., Seyyed Hossein Nasr and William Stoddart (Washington, DC: Foundation for Traditional Studies, 1991), 115.

Know to what extent the Creator has honoured you above all the rest of creation. The sky is not an image of God, nor is the moon, nor the sun, nor the beauty of the stars, nor anything of what can be seen in creation. You alone have been made the image of the Reality that transcends all understanding, the likeness of imperishable beauty, the imprint of true divinity, the recipient of beatitude, the seal of true light. When you turn to him you become that which he is himself. . . . There is nothing so great among beings that it can be compared with your greatness. God is able to measure the whole heaven with his span. *The earth and the sea are enclosed in the hollow of his hand. And although he is so great and holds all creation in the palm of his hand, you are able to hold him,* he dwells in you and moves within you without constraint. . . .[36]

According to esoteric teachings from many traditions, clearly reflected in the above passages, humanity is the "stem" connecting the earth to God. God sustains the earth and all that is in it only through man—a doctrine that is proved negatively by the fact that man alone has the power to destroy the earth: when we no longer take God as our center, and so depart from our own humanity, the earth begins to die. It is this truth, above all, that the aliens are doing all in their power to prevent us from remembering.

Nothing happens that is not God's will. Nonetheless, according to Sufi metaphysician Ibn al-'Arabi, even though all that happens is willed by God—because if it were possible for something contrary to His will to occur,

---

[36] *Second Homily on the Song of Songs* (PG 44, 765); italics mine. Quoted in *The Roots of Christian Mysticism,* by Olivier Clément (New York: New City Press, 1995), 79.

He would not be God—not everything is part of God's *wish*. This is why He sends us sacred laws, which let us know what to do and what to avoid if we want to come nearer to Him. Evil is not good in itself; it is contrary to God's wish. But he wills it—or, in Christian terms, allows it—as part of a greater good. We don't curse the worms that devour a dead body; and from a certain perspective the "aliens" are nothing but worms, whose job is to devour whatever is already dead in the human collective psyche. But that doesn't mean that it is a good idea to spend your time socializing with dead bodies; if you do, you will become ill. The experience of disease is a natural evil, and abduction, torture and rape are moral ones—which, to the victim, are nonetheless morally indistinguishable from natural disasters. Yet such evils, if we encounter them with a deep enough faith in our Creator, can sharpen our spiritual vigilance, and ultimately awaken us to a deeper Mercy. Just as lies testify to the Truth—not because they are true, but because the ability to recognize their falsehood is a sign of Truth's presence—so misfortune and catastrophe testify to Mercy. Even the worst sufferings can be known, God willing, as part of a Mercy which is so great that even this—even war, even cancer, even alien abduction—is swallowed up in it. As it says in the *ahadith qudsi*, "My Mercy precedeth my Wrath"; and in the Qur'an: *There is no refuge from God but in Him.*

Memoir & Conclusion

SINCE I HAVE CHOSEN to write about the UFO phenomenon, perhaps the reader is wondering whether I have any direct experience of the phenomenon myself. The answer is: in a small way, yes.

In the early 1970s, when my spiritual practice was entirely "experimental" and self-directed, I decided to do a spiritual retreat on Mt Shasta in northern California, a mountain sacred to the original Native American inhabitants, and also considered a "power spot" by every occultist, Neo-pagan, and New Age group under the sun. I traveled there with two friends, drove up the mountain as far as the road went, and then hiked in, arriving at Horse Camp, set in a sea of fragrant "Shasta tea" (pennyroyal), and high enough on the mountain to give a stunning, unobstructed view. For three days I ate nothing but brown rice, and also observed a vow of silence.

On one of the nights I spent on the mountain, I had a significant dream—perhaps my first "lucid dream" (a dream in which the dreamer "wakes up" to the fact that he is dreaming) since early childhood. In the dream I was gleefully aware that, since I was "only" dreaming, I could now do anything I wanted—though the ironic look on the face of the woman I met seemed to say, "yes, but not without consequences." (Only after a certain amount of hard experience in later years did I begin to understand the meaning of that look.)

One evening, shortly after the sun disappeared behind a distant range of mountains, I sat meditating, facing west. In those days I used to meditate with my eyes open, and this evening, as I slipped into a light trance, I saw two points of light crossing the western sky, from right to left. The light they gave off was somehow more precise, more defined, more "real" than ordinary light. (Spectrographic analysis of the light emanating from certain UFOs has since revealed it to be richer in various blended wavelengths of visible radiation than light from any known "natural" source.) As soon as I noticed them, I became alert, attentive; I rose out of trance, back to full waking consciousness—and the lights disappeared. Then I relaxed, centered my energy, sank back into a meditative state again: and there they were. I realized through this experience that UFOs habitually exist on a subtler plane of existence than the material—a plane which, however, is very close to the material and capable of impinging on it. The "craft" in question were not visible to my full waking consciousness, but neither were they a mental image. They existed in a layer of reality that somehow came between psychic and the material—what some have called the "etheric plane." (In later years I used the "etheric sight" I had began to develop during my retreat on Mt. Shasta to investigate—in other words, to meddle with— the world of the nature spirits.)

It is interesting that my one and only sighting of a UFO coincided with the first lucid dream of my adult life. (I continued to experience lucid dreaming and/or "astral projection" for years, and finally became involved in attempts to deliberately produce it, basing them partly on *Lucid Dreaming* by Dr Stephen LeBerge of Stanford University, as well as the books of Carlos Castaneda and Jane Roberts. It was only after my initiation into a traditional Sufi order that my lucid dream experiences finally stopped.) Lucid dreaming involves a partial erasure of the border between waking consciousness and dream consciousness, between material and psychic reality; the self-reflexive awareness of the waking state—or something similar to it—now has as its object not the world reported by the five senses but the subtle psychic environment.

All this was very interesting to me at the time. It seemed like a harmless excursion into the wonders of the etheric and psychic worlds, magical worlds where the Imagination ruled, and where that Imagination, in all its subjectivity, could finally be "objectively" validated. And if these worlds, at least to begin with, were "magical" to me more in the Walt Disney than in the Aleister Crowley sense of the word, I was to discover in later years that the heavy, humorless, and sinister aspects of these subtle planes could not ultimately be avoided.

Jumping ahead to November of the year 2003, I was interviewed on the syndicated radio program *A Closer Look*, hosted by Michael Corbin, on the subject of my book *The System of Antichrist: Truth and Falsehood in Postmodernism and the New Age*, from which some of the present book has been excerpted and revised. I don't know what he and our listeners may have learned from me, but I learned from him a very interesting thing: that, according to his own research, most of the people who claim to have been abducted by UFO aliens admit to having dabbled in the occult. Then, around a month later, I discovered on his website (in the archives of Corbin's programs) a report of a recent UFO sighting in Morehead, Kentucky. An investigator from MUFON (the Mutual UFO Network) was interviewed. She reported that a brilliant light had descended from the sky, shortly after which a woman's bloodcurdling screams were heard by several people in the area—though no missing person reports were filed and no one had as yet turned up whom the screams could be connected to. Cell phone trouble was also reported during the incident, and three electric clocks stopped permanently. Now, Morehead is where my wife's uncle lives with his wife and daughter; so she rang them up to ask if they had heard of the incident, and discovered that they lived only a stone's throw from the road where some of those who saw the UFO lived. Her aunt said she had neither witnessed nor heard of the sighting, but that ever since the date of the report, their own cell phones had been acting up.

So what I once thought of as harmless psychic entertainment—or, alternatively, as my first few serious steps on the spiritual Path—has now been revealed as a kind of uncanny terror, a terror striking all too close to home. As I have already pointed out, René Guénon, in *The Reign of Quantity and the Signs of the Times*, spoke of cracks in the Great Wall separating the material plane from the subtle plane as a sign of the approaching end of this cycle of manifestation, cracks that initially appear in the downward direction, producing a destructive influx of "infra-psychic" forces. And on reviewing the history of my own "explorations" of psychic worlds in the name of spiritual development, I am led to ask whether the very paradigm I had been operating on might be in some way related to this infra-psychic invasion.

The spiritual Path exists in an environment of Grace, specifically that initiatory Grace which the Sufis call *baraka*. Before we desire God, God must have desired us; both the initial call and the ultimate acceptance emanate from the pole of the Divine. Between this call and this acceptance, much work needs to be done by the spiritual traveler; yet the work is essentially the work of obedience, of active response to God's Grace. All that is needed to walk the path is given by God; our work is simply to assimilate what has been freely given.

The exact reverse of this is the paradigm of magic: Power is there, and it is up to us to break our way in to those worlds where power resides, to access it and use it. We can employ it (so the story goes) either to "take heaven by storm," or to obtain security, pleasure, and power in this world; what we use it for is entirely up to us. (In reality, of course, we cannot take heaven by storm, nor can we employ magic to fulfill our worldly desires without dire and most likely permanent consequences; see the Parable of the Wedding Feast in Matthew 22:1–14.) In any case, we must access power entirely on our own initiative. In the process we may tap "allies," "entities," "familiar spirits," who may guide us on our way, but their power to guide has nothing to do with any responsibility on our part to obey what is higher than us on the Great Chain of Being, to sacrifice our self-will in service to the Divine Will. These entities are more like repositories of useful information which we must struggle to contact and dominate, ultimately forcing them to divulge their secrets, by hook or by crook. And the program of "penetrating" the etheric and psychic planes, through various intense psycho-physical practices, as well as the use of psychedelic drugs, in order to explore them and make use of the energies they are composed of—and this certainly includes attempts to "control" the dream-state—is not spiritual practice: it is dark magic.

I now believe that it is largely the attempt by so many people today to penetrate the higher planes of existence from below, on the basis of a magical self-will, rather than responding obediently to a Grace descending from above, that widens those cracks in the Great Wall that are now opening in the downward direction. In other words, it is the magical will to break in to the higher worlds that allows infra-psychic, demonic forces to break in to this world from below.

The cold, sizzling, electrical energy of the UFO phenomenon (I'm speaking impressionistically here) seems specifically designed to devastate the nourishing emotional matrix of the human world—in other words, to destroy *love*. The Grace that descends from the higher worlds, and invites us to follow it—by God's own leave, and in His own time—is inseparable from love, precisely because God Himself *is* Love. The ripping away of our natural psychic protections on the other hand, the breaching of our psycho-physical energy fields so our vital and emotional energy can bleed away into uncanny, alien worlds, is the very opposite of love, though it is of the very essence of magic. [NOTE: Let anyone who wants a graphic portrayal of how magic destroys love, view the Russian motion picture *Shadows of our Forgotten Ancestors*.]

Like sexual promiscuity, the practice of dabbling in psychic and magical techniques may rupture the energetic and emotional self-containment that allows us to relate to others without losing our spiritual center, our inviolable human integrity; such "discretion" is a necessary part of self-respect, without which no love worthy of the name is possible. And if discretion is necessary for love to exist between human beings, it is all the more necessary in the relationship between the soul and God. The "co-dependency" exhibited by UFO abductees in relation to their abductors is nothing more than an especially intense case of the general lack of spiritual center exhibited by postmodern humanity.

If we do not know God, we cannot be ourselves; if we are not ourselves, we are dead meat for any entity from the infra-psychic realm who wants a slice of us. Buffy the Vampire Slayer would do better to practice the virtue of discretion, develop some basic self-respect, and learn to mind her own business. But this is effectively impossible without a fundamental faith in God, expressed through the ability to focus one's attention on Absolute Truth and Love. That is the only way the spooks and entities, the vampires and UFO aliens, who beset us in today's world can be definitively overcome: by starving them to death.

Those whose subtle attention has not yet awakened may still be relatively immune to the UFO influence— although as René Guénon says in *The Reign of Quantity*, the illusion of "ordinary life" which used to protect us from such incursions is fast breaking down. As for the rest of us, if our subtle attention is not reserved for God alone, it will be abducted, to one degree or another, by the forces of the infra-psychic. In other words, the perennial choice between obeying God and yielding to temptation is today being presented to us in a new guise: on the one hand, an attention to God that is both conscious and constant; on the other, an obsession with the demonic, usually unconscious, but in some cases conscious and deliberate. Our basic weapon against the alien invasion, then, is the spiritual practice known as *recollection*: the practice of gathering together the scattered energy of our subtle attention, withdrawing it from the many psychic worlds into which it has wandered, and placing it upon God alone.

Part II

UFOs, Mass Mind-Control,
&
The Saints of Satan

*

The Awliya al-Shaytan

UFOs, Mass Mind-Control
&
The Saints of Satan
(*The Awliya al-Shaytan*)

[Excerpted from *Vectors of the Counter-Initiation: The Course and Destiny of Inverted Spirituality*, 2012]

MY CENTRAL THESIS regarding the UFO phenomenon is as follows: UFO "aliens" are beings from another "dimension"—the world called in some systems the *etheric plane*, situated on the "isthmus" between the material world and the world of dreams and mental imagery. The etheric plane is home to the Jinn, the elemental spirits, the fairies, the powers of the air mentioned in Ephesians 2:2—"air" in this sense denoting the subtle-material dimension. (The "border" between the etheric plane and the world defined by the five senses apparently has something to do with the electromagnetic spectrum, as evidenced by the fact that the proximity of a UFO will often cause electronic equipment to malfunction.)

Some of the denizens of this world are best described as demons. Not all etheric "nations" are demonic, just as not every fish in shark-infested waters is a shark; nonetheless the early Christian Fathers were very wise to counsel strict avoidance of that realm, especially since those who most commonly interacted with it in their time—and are still doing so today—were (and are) the pagan magicians. The prime enigma is: How do the three aspects of the phenomenon relate to each other? Aren't they mutually exclusive? If UFOs are a real *physical* phenomenon, doesn't that mean that they have to be alien spaceships? If they are a *psychic* phenomenon, doesn't that mean that they *couldn't* be physical craft? And if the phenomenon is shown to be surrounded by human deception activities of the "Mission Impossible" variety, doesn't that mean the whole thing is a hoax?

No, on all three counts. Demons are subtle beings inhabiting the psychic or etheric plane who can *temporarily* materialize themselves and various objects in this world, but who cannot *remain* on our material plane in stable form for very long—if they could, they wouldn't have to *possess* people in order to work their evil in this world. (See Fr Seraphim Rose, *Orthodoxy and the Religion of the Future*.) As for "deception" perpetrated on humanity by certain groups, besides being attempts to piggyback on and use a phenomenon that the deceivers did not originate and cannot control (the same may perhaps be said for various human attempts to mimic alien "technology"), they may actually be (or *also* be) acts designed not simply to deceptively *imitate* the "aliens" in order to influence mass belief, but to actually *invoke* them, in line with the practice of "sympathetic magic" as described in the classic work on mythology and primitive belief, *The Golden Bough* by Sir James Frazer.

This depressing thesis leads us directly to the question of the possible involvement of the "intelligence community" and various arcane technologists, whose connections to the

UFO phenomenon have been well documented both by Jacques Vallee in *Messengers of Deception* and Peter Levenda in *Sinister Forces: A Grimoire of American Political Witch-craft*, who present it as outright satanism. (Levenda, for one, gives much well-researched evidence in support of this thesis.)

The case of pioneer rocket scientist Jack Parsons comes immediately to mind. Parsons was a follower of black magician Aleister Crowley and an associate of L. Ron Hubbard, another follower of Crowley who founded the Church of Scientology and who also (according to my correspondence with Beat Generation writer William Burroughs in the late 1960s, when Burroughs was in the process of breaking with Scientology) had a background in Naval Intelligence, something confirmed by Levenda.

According to Vallee, Parsons claimed to have met a "Venusian" in the Mojave Desert, performed pagan rituals at his launchings (as recounted by Levenda), and went on to co-found the Aerojet Corporation and the Jet Propulsion Laboratory. He provided early designs for the Pentagon building; a crater was named after him on the dark side of the moon. Parsons' rituals appear to be a continuation of a series of magical invocations performed by Crowley in 1918 called the "Amalantrah Workings," whose purpose was to open an interdimensional portal that would allow him access to beings from other worlds. One of the spooks that came through this portal was a generic or collective entity named "Lam." The sketch Crowley made of this being bears a striking resemblance to the "Gray"—the standard contemporary image of the extraterrestrial popularized by Whitley Strieber.

In light of these revelations, I believe we should take seriously Eastern Orthodox priest Fr Seraphim Rose's assertion, in *Orthodoxy and the Religion of the Future*, that the purpose of the great expansion of the UFO phenomenon after WWII was to lay the psychic groundwork for the advent of the regime of Antichrist, particularly since there is no question but that mass belief in UFOs, whether conceived of as alien spacecraft or as "interdimensional" manifestations, has been a key factor in the widespread pagan/occult revival that has so obviously weakened and undermined the world's religions.

French metaphysician René Guénon, author of *The Reign of Quantity and the Signs of the Times*, provides a solid metaphysical basis for the idea of Antichrist by demonstrating that this figure (whom Muslims call *al-Dajjal*, "the deceiver") is not simply a just-so fable that we must take on blind faith, but represents a necessary dialectical phase in the dissolution of the present cycle-of-manifestation, and the ultimate re-creation of the world. Guénon also provides a cosmological context for the UFO phenomenon, though he does not mention it by name, limiting himself to describing the breakthrough of "infra-psychic forces" due to the hardening of the cosmic environment under the regime of materialism (the phase he calls "Anti-Tradition"), followed by the psycho-physical fracturing of that environment in our own time (the phase of "Counter-Tradition," i.e., false religion).

As Guénon describes it, Anti-Tradition peaked in the nineteenth century under the regime of "classical materialism," while Counter-Tradition expresses itself in terms of our present postmodern worldview, one that might be termed "magical scientism." The upshot is that fissures are now starting to appear in the "great wall" separating the material world from the subtle-energy world, home to those beings that we regard, according to the scientistic paradigm, as "extra-terrestrial biological entities."

Fr Seraphim Rose, citing many of the Eastern Orthodox saints and the Greek Fathers, as well as Guénon himself, draws many exact parallels between the UFO phenomenon and the experiences of early Christian saints with the demonic powers, in the days when Christians were still a small minority within a largely pagan society, where the practice of magic was commonplace.

Jacques Vallee, in *Messengers of Deception* and his other books, provides much evidence to support this thesis, although he himself does not assert it; and if Peter Levenda's well-documented findings are accurate (findings that demonstrate massive cross-pollenization since WWII between the military, the intelligence community, and the power elite on the one hand, and the world of magicians and the occultists on the other), we can say without fear of exaggeration that elements of the CIA and the "military-industrial complex" are involved in practices that can be accurately described as satanism, whether or not they go by that name.

If Jack Parsons, as Levenda shows, identified himself with Antichrist and dedicated himself to the destruction of Christianity, and if prominent psychic researcher Andrija Puharich, with all his connections to the intelligence community, was involved in channeling so-called "extra-terrestrial intelligences," for which read "the powers of the air" (see below), is Seraphim Rose's thesis (and mine) really that far-fetched? It will only seem so to those who do not accept the reality of the paranormal.

In his book *The Nine* (the first in the *Sinister Forces* trilogy), Levenda provides hard documentary evidence in support of many conclusions I myself had earlier reached, based mostly upon intuition and logic, and supported by only a few pieces of data I took as factual. For example, when I considered the information provided by Jacques Vallee that the UFO phenomenon is physical *and* psychic *and* also sometimes a product of human deception, I simply drew a logical inference: that if it is both psychic and physical, it might well be a *materialization* (usually short-lived) of psychic realities in the form of physical objects and events, such as magicians have always reputedly been able to produce. And if it is also surrounded by activities of human deception, I asked myself if such activities, at least on one level, might be *invocations* designed to *catalyze* these very materializations.

Such activities constitute in fact the basic premise of the practice of "sympathetic magic" that was universal in the ancient world, and in the world of primitive tribes up to our own time: that in order to produce a phenomenon, the magician (after preparing suitable conditions) *imitates* it, as a Voudoo practitioner will stick pins in a doll so as to injure the person it represents. Anyone who has handled or bought a "rain stick" at their local health food store or Pagan Shoppe has come into contact with a traditional tool of sympathetic magic.

I then further conjectured that certain magicians found they were able to produce *actual* preternatural phenomena through autosuggestion. As with the Tibetan practice of psychically materializing a *tulpu*, their ability to alter their psychic state also ultimately altered their physical environment as well, which is the premise of all magic. And then, in the early twentieth century, as studies of the effect of propaganda on entire "radio age" populations became better known, certain black magicians came to an obvious and horrible conclusion: that if changing their own consciousness could produce *local* manifestations of the preternatural, changing the consciousness of the masses could produce *global ones*. (The *mass* dissemination of LSD, likely sponsored by the CIA as part of their MK-ULTRA mind-control program, might well have been an expression of this agenda.)

Consequently, the "cracks in the great wall" were pried wide open, and in flew the UFOs and all the other spooks and demons and sinister forces that beset postmodern humanity. Certainly, such entities have a long history of intervention in our world, but today's *mass interest* and belief in them, and *mass experience* of them, has probably not been so widespread since late antiquity.

Perhaps it was the Nazis, who, as Peter Levenda demonstrates in his book *Unholy Alliance*, placed all of Germany and much of Europe under the power of a satanic cult dedicated to invoking the Powers of Darkness, first got those Powers' foot firmly in the door in terms of the modern world. This would explain the "foo-fighters" (early "flying saucers") encountered by the allied air forces in their bombing runs over the dying Reich. After all, the literal meaning of *holocaust* is mass immolation of human victims in the cult of a pagan god. And as Argentine writer Jorge Luis Borges pointed out in his story "Deutches

Requiem," the Nazis not only immolated the Jews but ultimately offered Germany itself as a living sacrifice on the altar they raised to the birth of the New Man and the New Age of Darkness. And we might as well mention that certain of the secret "experimental aircraft," some of them disc-shaped, produced by the Nazis, and later by the Americans, during and after the war (recalling that the United States "inherited" many Nazi scientists through Operation Paperclip) were probably attempts to imitate the aeronautical capabilities exhibited by UFOs, on the theory that these were highly-advanced technological devices built either by the human enemy or an extraterrestrial race. But some of the more "esoteric" of those involved in their production may have understood them on a different level: as another instance of sympathetic magic, one more highly concrete act of *invocation.*

As Levenda has amply demonstrated, Jack Parsons was at the center of all these vectors of dark force: scientist, close associate of intelligence agents, pagan magician. He is one of the ones who let the cat out of the bag in terms of the possibility of a literal synthesis between satanism and modern science. But an even more interesting cat is the one released by Harold Dahl, Fred Crisman, and Kenneth Arnold.

The story, recounted in Levenda's *The Nine,* is as follows: On June 21, 1947, harbor patrolman Harold Dahl spotted six UFOs hovering over his boat anchored at Maury Island in Puget Sound, this being the first major civilian UFO sighting after WWII. A slight explosion occurred on one of the objects, after which hot metal rained down upon and damaged Dahl's boat, killing his dog and injuring his teenage son. He had a camera on board and was able to photograph the objects. After returning with his boat to Tacoma he told his boss, Fred Crisman, of the strange event, and turned over to him his camera, the photographs, and a sample of the metallic slag that had fallen from the sky. (More than 20 years after this event, Crisman was subpoenaed by Jim Garrison in the course of his investigation of the Kennedy assassination, and was found to be an ex-OSS officer with CIA connections, as well as a friend of Clay Shaw!)

The next evening, Harold Dahl was visited by the twentieth century's first recorded "man in black," who advised him to forget the whole incident. The following day Crisman went to Maury Island, retrieved some more of the material that had fallen on Dahl's boat, and spotted another UFO. A day later, on June 24, one Kenneth Arnold, a deputy federal marshal and member of an Idaho search and rescue team, while piloting his aircraft near Mt. Ranier in Washington State in search of a missing transport plane, spotted nine UFOs flying in formation. His subsequent description of them gave us our term "flying saucer"; it was these two sightings that initiated the first American "saucer scare" of the postwar era.

Arnold's account was published in an Oregon newspaper; then, in early July, he was visited by two Air Force intelligence officers from California who were interested in hearing his story. Next, Fred Crisman contacted Raymond Palmer, editor of *Amazing Stories* magazine, with Harold Dahl's story of the Maury Island encounter, but not before Palmer himself got in touch with Kenneth Arnold about the Mt. Ranier sighting and suggested that

Arnold meet with Dahl, a meeting that took place in Tacoma on July 30.

Flying to make that meeting on July 29, Arnold saw another, larger fleet of UFOs. And when he arrived in Tacoma, found that no hotel rooms were available except for a room in the most expensive hotel in town that had already been reserved in his name by person or persons unknown. Arnold and Dahl came together in that room to compare notes about their strange experiences, after which United Press International apparently received a verbatim transcript of the entire meeting!

So, Harold Dahl was visited by his "man in black" a mere 24 hours after his UFO sighting and the explosion that killed his dog—and this at a time when UFOs did not loom large in the public mind, as they certainly were to do in short order, due in great part to the revelations of Dahl and Arnold themselves. How is this to be explained? In the absence of any mass paranoia about UFOs, why would a presumptive government agency *already* have in place a system seemingly designed to suppress evidence for the existence of extraterrestrials? After all, that evidence had not yet appeared, at least to the public at large. And though it may be true that the government and the intelligence community feared that the open appearance of such evidence was imminent and had taken steps to cushion the blow of these revelations on the public mind, another and equally logical explanation is that the man in black and his superiors *knew that the UFO apparition over Maury Island was about to take place.* And they could only have known this, (1) if they themselves produced the phenomenon, or (2) if they were in touch with those entities who planned to, and had received advance warning. Since it strains credulity to believe that any terrestrial technology available at that time, or even today, could have produced fleets of craft that were both undeniably physical objects and also capable of feats no human aircraft could remotely duplicate, one *logical* (which certainly does not mean *conventional*) explanation is that the beings in control of those craft had communicated with their human agents to the effect that: "We are going to appear at such and such a place on such and such a date; get ready to put into action the follow-up plan we discussed."

Likewise, the mysterious advance booking of the hotel room where Kenneth Arnold met with Harold Dahl, the apparent bugging of their room, and the release of the transcripts of their conversation to UPI, are all extremely good evidence in support of the hypothesis that both Dahl's and Arnold's UFO sightings were somehow pre-arranged or known about in advance; for if this were not the case, how could such a well-designed plan to exploit their reactions to those sightings, obviously requiring extensive resources and a great deal of coordinated effort, have been put into action so soon after the events themselves?

One point on which I disagree with Peter Levenda is where he assumes that the appearance of the "man in black" to Dahl, and the recording and release of Dahl's and Arnold's conversation in the hotel room, were part of an effort to *discredit* their reports. Certainly, the threats made by the "man" would make anyone think twice about revealing what he'd seen, but could this messenger's appearance not be equally well explained as an attempt to *lend credibility* to those reports? What could be more likely to convince someone of the reality and serious import of a particular experience than a threat by a mysterious stranger of unfortunate consequences if that experience were ever revealed? And why leak the conversation of Dahl and Arnold to the *UPI itself* unless the intent behind the leak was, not to debunk UFOs, but to influence the public to believe in them? [NOTE: *It was apparently decided in 2021 that the widespread "unofficial" belief in UFOs had been well-enough cultivated on a covert level to ensure that an about-face by the government toward an open admission of the reality of the phenomenon would be generally accepted.*]

A major *myth* of the UFO belief-system is that "the government knows everything, or at least an awful lot, about UFOs, but is hiding all this data from us because it wants to convince us that UFOs—which are probably extraterrestrial—don't really exist." One way mind-control works, however, is through the implanting of *assumptions* like this into the public psyche. Beliefs that, because they deal with the fringes of consensus reality, are rarely subjected to logical analysis, often become the focus of both "true belief" and "cynical debunking"—two equal and opposite departures from logical objectivity, two sides of the same coin. And to the degree that the effort to make sense of the UFO phenomenon is limited to the question "are they real or only an illusion?," all questions of their spiritual *quality* or their possible *use* as a vector of mass mind-control are pushed into the background. You are either a true believer or a cynical debunker; the purpose of the cynical debunker is in fact to *create* the true believer, to separate the knowledge that he or she possesses of the reality of the UFO phenomenon—based on painstaking research if not personal experience—from the collective validation such knowledge would normally enjoy, thus producing a state of *paranoia*.

Undoubtedly, those working to influence mass belief well know that an individual laboring under this kind of oppression will desperately seek to overcome his schizophrenic split from consensus reality by finding, or developing, an explanation for his experience that consensus reality will accept. Consequently, he or she will be apt to accept uncritically whatever explanations the social engineers may for their own purposes wish to provide (see my account of the mind-control technique of "deferred closure" below). And just as the cynical debunker causes the true believer to harden his position, so the believer has the same effect on the debunker.

As we shall see later on in extensive detail, Harvard psychiatrist, UFOlogist, and Pulitzer Prize-willing author John Mack (he won his Pulitzer for a book on T. E. Lawrence, who was a British Intelligence asset; his UFO book is entitled *Abduction*), gained influence over his clients (most of them "alien abductees") by *taking their side* against their cynical friends, relatives, and employers, many of whom thought they were crazy. But Dr. Mack was their "friend"; Dr. Mack *believed* them. His job was to help them *accept* their experiences—"accept" them as real, certainly, but also "accept" the terroristic violation and *indoctrination* such experiences usually involved—two *very* different meanings of the same word. Mack's job, apparently, was to solidify and exploit the alien control that first penetrated the souls of his clients during their abduction experience, in a perfect example of the well-known brainwashing technique of alternating terror (the abducting, violating aliens) with relief (the helpful, understanding Dr. Mack).

✳

There has definitely been a concerted government effort to *debunk* the reality of UFOs; I certainly don't want to deny this obvious fact. But as I have stated, I believe there has also been a *parallel* attempt to *plant* the idea of their reality into the public mind. It is possible that these seemingly opposed efforts may represent different factions within the power elite, but it is equally possible that both are part of a single overall strategy.

In the well-known 1997 UFO documentary *Area 51*, one of the interviewees makes the claim that as the human race entered the space age, the U.S. government and the military confronted the following question: What if in our exploration of space we encounter intelligent, technologically-advanced aliens and establish their reality? What effect would this have on human society? The conclusion was that it would create social chaos. So the Rand Corporation and the Brookings Institution were hired to develop a plan to head off this potential chaos. The result was a proposal that the public be *slowly acclimatized* to the notion of human encounter with extraterrestrial aliens over a 30-year period. Clearly, the planting of evidence (spurious or otherwise) pointing to the reality of aliens, and the debunking of evidence in favor of that reality, would both find their place in such a plan.

So here is the big question: *what was supposed to happen at the end of those 30 years?* The Rand/Brookings social engineering plan may or may not actually exist, but if it does, it could have started out as described, then progressively morphed into a plan to *produce* incontrovertible evidence of alien/human interaction (spurious or otherwise) after the 30 years were up, for specific social engineering purposes—perhaps to create the "united earth" that must ready itself to encounter an enemy from another galaxy. This, incidentally, would go a long way toward explaining the heavy and undisguised military and intelligence involvement in the Disclosure Movement (see below). As Peter Levenda further recounts in *The Nine*, the relationship between the UFO phenomenon and the push for a One-World Government was clearly expressed by General Douglas MacArthur in his speech to the cadets at West Point on May 12,1962.

[*The following excerpt from his speech was already quoted in the Introduction to this book, but due to its central importance it wouldn't hurt to quote it again*]:

> We deal now, not with the things of this world alone, but with the illimitable distances and as yet unfathomed mysteries of the universe . . . of ultimate conflict between a *united human race* and *the sinister forces of some other planetary galaxy*; of such dreams and fantasies as to make life the most exciting of all times. And through all this welter of change and development your mission remains fixed, determined, inviolable. It is to win our wars.

Returning now to *Area 51*, I would suggest that anyone who is able to obtain this documentary should direct his or her attention to one scene where, in a supposed video of a UFO, the object in question is described by the narrator as entering the field of vision "from the lower right," whereas the actual image we see is in the upper half of the screen. This disconnect between word and image is one form of the mind control technique I have named "subliminal contradiction." If the viewer accepts both the message received by his eyes and the opposite message received through his ears unconsciously, without noting the contradiction, his critical faculties are at least partially disabled and he becomes highly receptive to suggestion. (The "lower right quadrant" element also suggests a Neuro-Linguistic Programming technique.) This "error" in the documentary does not appear in the (supposedly unrehearsed) accounts of the interviewees; it appears in the composed narrative of the voice-over—and if it were an actual error it would certainly have been caught and corrected in the editing process. So we must conclude that it was deliberate, and thus that *Area 51* as a whole is a mind control production, possibly to further prepare us for the "disclosure" to come.

As for the revelation (if legitimate) that Rand and Brookings produced a report recommending that the belief in UFOs be slowly engineered into the public mind, this could be an example of the mind-control technique Michael Hoffman calls "revelation of the method," designed to take the wind out of the sails of the whistle-blowers and investigative reporters by glibly admitting what these dedicated researchers have spent their lives vainly trying to prove, as if all their struggle and sacrifice were meaningless, as if their smug adversaries were now so sure of their dominance that they no longer felt the need to conceal even their most outrageous crimes. It could also be a way of de-potentiating any evidence of social engineering projects related to UFOs by admitting that the promotion of a belief in alien visitations had indeed been going on, but for an entirely benign purpose: "Certainly we are covertly promoting the belief in UFOs—not to delude you, however, but to prepare you to accept *the truth.*" (This assertion appears not only in *Area 51*, but in the 2000 documentary *Close Encounters: Proof of Alien Contact*, which I also accessed through Netflix.) And to both promote and debunk the existence of alien-human contact could certainly represent the technique of "subliminal contradiction" applied on a mass level. This technique even seems to form part of MacArthur's speech in 1962: what could be more contradictory than for the cadets at West Point to be asked to steel themselves to fulfill a "fixed, determined, inviolable" mission in a war against "fantasies and dreams"?

As I have already made clear, I entirely accept the reality of the UFO phenomenon and the existence of "aliens." However, I see these aliens essentially as demons, as well as accepting the possibility that certain elements of the military and intelligence communities might have established ongoing contact with these entities, whether or not they fully recognized their demonic nature—an alliance that could have begun in some cases (as Peter Levenda and others have speculated) when scientists in Russia or at the Stanford Research Institute or the Lawrence Livermore Laboratory inadvertently "broke through" in the course of their various psycho-technological tinkerings into the dimension the demons inhabit. (See *The Manson Secret*, the third book in the *Sinister Forces* trilogy, for accounts of the harrowing preternatural apparitions that dogged the scientists from Lawrence Livermore after they undertook to test the psychic powers, including psychokinesis, of famous Israeli psychic Uri Geller in 1974–1975.) And it is conceivable that such experiments in arcane science could have been inspired, in some cases at least, by the demons themselves. It is also possible, however, that stories of ongoing contact between extraterrestrials and the U.S. government, such as those reported by Prof. Michael Salla's Exopolitics Institute, represent an attempt on the part of the military and/or the intelligence community to co-opt elements of the UFO community, turning them (if possible) from relentless critics into loyal supporters of "federal UFO policy."

"Mind-control" techniques of various descriptions also operate in ordinary social situations. Anyone who has a basically manipulative way of relating to others is, if successful, a junior grade mind-controller; such people often gravitate to intelligence work, where they can hone their skills and bring them to a more professional level. I personally experienced the effects of the "revelation of the method" technique at the hands of a "friend" with whom I was involved in a certain church project. For quite a few years this man had been a management consultant with an impressive portfolio of past work in the world of multinational corporations, teaching various meditative and cognitive techniques to upper management and applying them to conflict resolution and organizational development; his ex-wife had a background in undercover work with the Pinkerton Detective Agency. On one occasion I told him, "I feel like I'm being used"—to which he replied: "But you *want* to be used, don't you? Don't you want to be *useful?*" Today my answer to that question would simply be "no—at least not by, or to, you"; but at that time I only replied, "Uh, yeah, sure, I guess…" In like manner, when Americans are told "your mass consciousness is being manipulated—but you already suspected that, didn't you?" our answer often is not "You bastard, are *you* one of the manipulators?" but "Hey! We were right!"—a much pleasanter sentiment, a much less frightening concept, than the idea of total helplessness.

✳

Since my main area of expertise is traditional metaphysics, let us now take a look at how various mind-control techniques, or those events and processes I believe might represent them, would look from a metaphysical perspective.

To begin with, the use of the "revelation of the method" technique to demoralize the public by nonchalantly letting them know that they are (perhaps) under total control, is in fact based on a satanic inversion of the metaphysical principle that God is both Absolute Good and Absolute Power, an inversion that produces the counter-proposition: *whatever is inevitable must therefore be good*—the same principle that leads some voters to "back the winner" even if he or she is opposed to everything they claim to hold sacred.

And subliminal contradiction itself is in turn the satanic inversion of another metaphysical principle, which holds that "God is beyond the *dvandvas*, the pairs-of-opposites." To employ subliminal contradiction is thus to imply that whatever reality may lie *beyond* the contradiction ("the truth is out there!" as the *X-Files* mantra has it) must *necessarily* be Absolute Truth and Absolute Power.

These inversions of universally accepted metaphysical principles are so precise and so word-perfect that one is led to ask whether or not certain satanists, or mind-controllers trained and employed by the military or the intelligence services, may have in fact studied metaphysics so as to put it to use—in inverted mode—as the highest form of the "magical" manipulation of consciousness. Anyone who has read *The Screwtape Letters* by C. S. Lewis will be familiar with the idea of the demonic manipulation of mass social attitudes—a manipulation that we might ascribe, under the theory that devils are rebel angels, to the "fallen cherubim." The cherubs appear in the Book of Ezekiel as flying-saucer-like aerial wheels whose rims are studded with eyes, symbolizing an *aeonian* knowledge that is both global in space and simultaneous in time. And the inverted, satanic metaphysicians who may be inspired by these fallen cherubim could well be those to whom René Guénon, in *The Reign of Quantity and the Signs of the Times*, applies the Islamic/Sufic name of *Awliya al-Shaytan*, "saints of satan."

I would also like to draw attention to what I believe could be another mind-control technique that appears from time to time in the various UFO videos available on YouTube. A video with a caption like "Huge Amazing Mothership Appears over El Paso!" is followed by a video of a sky with clouds, and nothing else. This is similar to subliminal contradiction, but is also apparently an attempt to *suggest* that the viewer sees something that he in fact does not see—in other words, to set up a hallucination. (It would be interesting to know whether subliminal images form a part of this process.)

This technique is also based on an inversion of a particular metaphysical principle that lies at the heart of Christian theology, in this case the principle that God the Father, Who is Reality Itself, is invisible ("None has seen the Father at any time," said Jesus in John 1:18). In other words, the UFO that is invisible, but *actually* there, is identified with God Himself—the corollary being (again in Christian terms) that a UFO that *does* appear is equivalent to Christ, who is the *manifestation* or *icon* of the Father. And a UFO that is considered equivalent to Christ is nothing less than a sign of the Antichrist.

✳

Whatever one may make of the above observations, I in any case believe the evidence is quite strong that elements of the U.S. government and the governments of other nations have been doing all they can to implant the idea of the reality of UFOs as extraterrestrial spacecraft in the public mind, while *simultaneously* debunking this belief. Why else would Douglas MacArthur have come right out and told us in 1962 that the next world war—or the next "war of the worlds"—will be between a *united humanity* and invaders from *another galaxy*? In doing so, he may have in fact revealed that the ultimate goal served by the inculcation of a belief in extraterrestrials in the public mind is to create a One-World Government by uniting the peoples of the earth against a (real or imagined) common enemy—a speculation Jacques Vallee also put forward in *Messengers of Deception*. And if a united earth is the goal of such propaganda and mind-control, it stands to reason that the impetus and resources necessary to carry on such a massive campaign of social engineering—which I believe includes the production of such motion pictures as *ET* and *Close Encounters of the Third Kind*, (both directed by Steven Spielberg), the docudrama *Roswell*, and television series like *The X-Files*, as well as well-timed public releases of classified UFO files by the governments of Mexico, France, the UK, and more recently both New Zealand and the UK a second time—likely emanate from a power bloc that transcends the national governments.

In the section "Mind Control and Roswell: The Spielberg Agenda?" from *Cracks in the Great Wall* (2005), which makes up Part I of this book, I commented on the mind-control-like qualities of Spielberg's UFO productions. I subsequently learned from *Sinister Forces* that a nuclear physicist named Jack Sarfatti, a colleague of psychic investigator Andrija Puharich, and also of Uri Geller, was not only involved in the "remote viewing" experiments at the Stanford Research Institute (a group that also studied the powers of Geller), experiments that involved the U.S. Army, the CIA, the NSA, the DIA, and the National Security Council, but on one occasion introduced Uri Geller to Steven Spielberg! So it would seem that a U.S. intelligence influence operating through some of Spielberg's movies is not at all beyond the realm of possibility. [*NOTE: In an email from Tom DeLonge to the Hillary Clinton campaign on the subject of UFOs, accessed by Edward Snowden and available through Wikileaks, DeLonge references Spielberg as someone who was invited to attend his meetings with Podesta.*]

Several motion pictures beyond those produced by Spielberg appear to be attempts to construct and manipulate the "alien" myth. Leaving aside the more obvious candidates for this role, such as *The Day the Earth Stood Still*, the 1952 science fiction movie *Red Planet Mars*, directed by Harry Horner and produced by Anthony Veiller (who also wrote the screenplay), seems to fit this description. It is interesting from a synchronistic point of view that the motion picture was released the same year that massive UFO fleets made their appearance over Washington, DC. Even more interesting is the fact that the *The Day the Earth Stood Still*, screenplay by Edmund H. North (who made training films for the U.S. Army Signal Corps during the Second World War), was released a year earlier; it certainly seems to have predicted (if not actually catalyzed) the DC sightings.

Red Planet Mars presents itself as a simplistic piece of Cold War propaganda with a rather absurd plot—but an entirely different text is evident just beneath the surface. During World War II, Horner worked on a U.S. Air Force propaganda film by Moss Hart called *Wingéd Victory*, based on Hart's play of the same name. Simultaneously, Veiller was working with Frank Capra on several films in the documentary/propaganda film series entitled *Why We Fight*. When Horner made his directorial debut with *Red Planet Mars*, starring Peter Graves, this got him in on the ground floor of an American postwar trend, or program, of using science fiction movies to posit new social paradigms and belief-systems, movies sometimes drawing upon the expertise of WWII cinematic propagandists trying to reinvent themselves in a Cold War context, possibly under continued government patronage. All of them were following more or less in the footsteps of H.G. Wells.

The basic story-line is as follows: An independent American scientist begins sending radio messages to Mars and picking up replies suggesting intelligent life; these exchanges are also being monitored by a Nazi scientist in South America working for the Russian Communists. The communiqués, detailing the advanced technology and high quality of life on the Red Planet, cause global chaos and economic breakdown, especially in the West, which in turn leads Russia and the Soviet Block to believe they have won the Cold War. But then messages with a religious content begin arriving, messages suggesting that God, or Christ, is the "supreme ruler" or "supreme being" of Mars. (The Mormons actually hold a similar belief.) This precipitates a worldwide religious revival, which the President of the United States interprets as heralding the advent of a new universal faith, based on the most ancient truths, one that encompasses and transcends all the traditional religions. This revival culminates in a Christian uprising in Russia that overthrows the Soviet system and installs the Russian Orthodox Patriarch of Moscow as the new Head of State. The world rejoices.

All this appears on the surface to be simply another example of the "Christian anti-Communism" of the Cold War; but since the religious world revolution is shown as based on the revelation that Jesus is not God, but really only a Martian—leading to the inescapable conclusion that there is no God—it is obvious that a radically different worldview and agenda are being promoted here: what seems a Christian revolution against dialectical materialism is really a *materialist* revolution against every religious faith—and the new universalist religion based on ancient truth is clearly the regime of Antichrist.

Then things take a turn: the Nazi scientist shows up at

the American scientist's laboratory, and reveals that he was the one who transmitted the messages supposedly coming from Mars. He shows them the original texts in his notebook; he threatens to tell the world of his deception and destroy the new-found peace. The American scientist and his wife realize that the later religious messages are not in the notebook, so they must have come from another source. At this point the American scientist begins to "lose his faith in Mars" and believe that the messages might have been a deception planted by the U.S. government to bring down the Soviet system. The Nazi agrees.

The film now reaches a Luciferian/nihilist crescendo. The Nazi starts quoting Milton's "Paradise Lost": "Better to reign in Hell than serve in Heaven . . . the unconquerable Will,/And study of revenge, immortal hate,/And courage never to submit or yield..."; he declares straight-out that he worships Lucifer. Then, unbeknownst to the Nazi, the American scientist releases explosive gas into the laboratory, planning to blow him up along with himself and his wife in order to preserve the deception that has brought peace to the world. His wife sees what he has done, agrees to die with him, tells him she loves him, and says that what they are doing is good.

The Nazi still doesn't realize what is afoot, but pulls a gun and holds them captive. The scientist's wife asks him to light a cigarette for her, which will touch off the explosion, but he resists. She says to the Nazi, immediately after she has chosen to commit murder and double suicide in order to protect a global deception: "God gave us free will, that's what distinguishes us from the animals. But if we choose evil now, that's the end of the human story." The

Nazi realizes that the room is filled with explosive gas and struggles to prevent the American from lighting his lighter, but at the last moment a *real* message starts coming in from Mars, indicating that the earlier religious messages were genuine, so the Americans no longer need to blow up the laboratory. The Nazi, however, in an attempt to suppress the message, fires at the transmitter, and the laboratory blows up anyway, killing all three.

The eulogy for the scientist and his wife is delivered by the President of the United States, who talks about their being caught up to God in a fiery chariot (the lab explosion), but then contradicts himself, rather eerily, by saying "the whole earth is their sepulcher." Apparently, no more messages will be coming from Mars because only the dead couple (and the Nazi) knew how to receive them.But the last message has been preserved: "Ye have done well, ye good and faithful servant." The movie ends with a view of churches all over the globe filled with the faithful giving thanks to God for their salvation in a world of peace. In the last scene a Pentagon general embraces the American scientist's two orphan sons, as if he were their father now. The whole idea that Jesus was a Martian is never denied, just drowned and suppressed in a wave of "Christian" piety.

So, here we see God's salvation of the world identified with murder and suicide, perhaps in a Luciferian inversion of the Crucifixion and the suicide of Judas; we see the "good" American scientist and his wife, and the "evil" Nazi, united in choosing to commit a capital crime and mortal sin; we see *telling the truth to the world* associated with Nazi *evil*, and *deceiving the world* identified with upstanding American Christian (or upstanding American

Martian) *good*; and we see the military taking over the protection and raising of our children.

The effect of this motion picture, in terms of social engineering, is to deny the existence of God but retain religious sentiments—while diverting them to an inappropriate, material object (i.e., an idol)—and to represent deception and crime as the *only* way to world peace and global unity: if the people would only forget God, make a god out of science, happily let themselves to be deceived, and call evil good, all would be well on planet earth.

I have no doubt whatsoever that these are the precise social engineering goals of some in the power elite, who may well have hired the propaganda-film makers Horner and Veiller (who had already worked under their direction during the war) to implant these notions in the mass mind, under cover of cheap cinematic fiction that need not be rigorously analyzed because it is not expected to be taken seriously.

✳

Postwar cinema presents us with two basic images of the "extraterrestrials": they are depicted either as a technologically advanced and spiritually enlightened race whose intentions toward humanity are good, or as a race of evil monsters bent on enslaving or destroying us. *Red Planet Mars*, *The Day the Earth Stood Still*, Carl Sagan's *Contact*, and (in some ways) Steven Spielberg's *Close Encounters of the Third Kind*, present more-or-less the first view—although *The Day the Earth Stood Still* portrays the aliens as interstellar policemen who will destroy us if we do not renounce war, as they have—except, apparently, when they opt to destroy entire races and planets from time to time. On the other hand, *The War of the Worlds*, the television miniseries *V*, *Independence Day*, and a whole slew of grade B space operas, present the aliens as enemies of the human race.

However, both these versions of the aliens have one thing in common: they both call for *global unity*, either as the crowning "evolutionary" achievement of humanity as helped and guided by the "space brothers," or (as Douglas MacArthur warned us) the necessary "united front" against an enemy from beyond the stars. And given the nature of the mind-control technique I have named "unconscious contradiction," it is not inconceivable that both views of the space aliens were designed to work together. In any case, they *do* work together *de facto*.

It is quite likely that H. G. Wells, as a Fabian Socialist and an unashamed technocratic globalist, intended his *War of the Worlds* as a propaganda-piece promoting global unity; he certainly presents space travel as part and parcel of a politically united earth in his *Things to Come*. In the first book he paints the aliens as enemies of the earth; in the second, it is the higher caste of technocratic globalists who initiate space travel, as against the bigotry and super-stition of the ignorant masses who want humanity to remain earthbound. In *The Day the Earth Stood Still* the aliens act as a sort of United Nations peacekeeping force; in *Red Planet Mars* and *Contact* they are revealed as the actual *material* reality behind the human belief in God. But despite their differences, every one of these motion pictures is a clear *apology for political globalization.*

The question I keep asking myself but cannot answer with certainty (but that definitely needs answering) is:

could this unanimity be nothing more than an accidental reflection of the *zeitgeist*, or is it, at least in part, the product of a deliberate program of social engineering?

A more recent example of this kind of engineering is the book *Challenges of Change* (2008) by "retired NORAD officer" Stanley A. Fulham, which is supposed to be based on revelations made by an "intelligence officer connected with NORAD" of a great deal of UFO information that has been kept secret from the public by the U.S. government, and which predicted that UFOs would appear in the skies above earth's cities on Oct. 13 of 2010, in a sort of real-life version of a similar episode from science fiction writer Arthur C. Clarke's book *Childhood's End*. The UFOs dutifully appeared, right on schedule (the videos were posted on YouTube), although the ones that showed up in the sky above New York's Central Park gave more the impression of illuminated helium balloons than of the more spectacular and convincing types of UFO phenomena.

Retired astronaut Edgar Mitchell, in a 2008 interview, made a "startling new revelation" about UFOs, claiming that the U.S. government has been trying to hide their existence for years, but that despite their best efforts the truth finally leaked out. He also revealed that he had been briefed by the Pentagon on several occasions (one of these briefings, he implied, being fairly recent) to the effect that the UFO phenomenon is real, and the government is in ongoing contact with the extraterrestrials. We know, however, that Mitchell has been making claims like this for many years; so why would the Pentagon reveal to him information they hoped would never be made public when, judging by his past statements, he was all but certain to make it public—as he in fact did? And why was he never subject to persecution or legal action for revealing classified information? This makes no sense—unless the *true* intent of the unknown source of this "information" (and of Mitchell himself), is to implant the belief in UFOs in the public mind. As Levenda points out, Edgar Mitchell (who also happens to be a Freemason) has a long-standing involvement in paranormal research; he was the one who was on hand to welcome Uri Geller to the Stanford Research Institute.

One of the methods employed in this mass social engineering campaign is illustrated by the following anecdote: *Someone admitted to an American Air Force base catches a glimpse of an object resembling a UFO through an open hangar door. As soon as he sees it, the door is closed and he is told "You weren't supposed to see that." Then, a few days later, the proverbial "men in black" arrive at his house, threatening reprisals if he tells anyone what he saw.*

This is a classic case of psychological manipulation, where an event that might have made little impression on him, suddenly, through the use of terror, assumes the status of a dark revelation: "If these people are desperate enough to threaten to harm me or my family if I reveal what I know, THEN WHAT I SAW MUST BE REAL."

✳

So it appears that various governments, possibly taking their orders from an authority that transcends the national state, have been trying to capitalize on the UFO phenomenon by *officially* denying that it exists (against massive and mounting evidence) while at the same clandestinely leaking stories confirming that it does exist. Why would they do this, other than as an opportunity to employ the subliminal contradiction technique on a mass level, or as a way of "easing" the public into an acceptance of the reality of extraterrestrials so as to minimize social chaos when the big "disclosure" arrives?

For one thing, if they were to officially admit the existence of the UFO phenomenon, they would either have to say "we don't know what it is and we can't control it"—thus undercutting their own authority—or they would have to produce the alien diplomats they are claiming to be in contact with so they could appear on the Oprah show. Since they can't produce those diplomats, they would rather let a growing segment of the population believe that they *are* in contact with extraterrestrials, but that they must hide this to prevent mass panic. By acting in this way, they are suggesting to the populace that they have immensely powerful allies, and at the same time preventing their lack of a full understanding of the UFO phenomenon (which Jacques Vallee believes to be the case) from being publicly exposed. So what we may have is a mass mind-control project piggybacking on a real phenomenon—which would explain why some UFO encounters are truly inexplicable, while others appear to be deceptions most likely produced by human action. [NOTE: *As of 2021, however, the technology necessary to produce a convincing simulacrum of an alien ambassador may exist, or be in development.*]

This social engineering program already appears to have produced, among other things, the *Disclosure Movement*, many of whose sponsors have military or intelligence backgrounds, which is dedicated to pressuring the U.S.

government to come clean on what it knows about UFOs and alien contact. And every time they "force" the government to reveal another item of data about the "reality" of this contact, the greater their sense of triumph after so many years of social marginalization, of being typed as mentally imbalanced cranks. In view of this long-delayed "success," it is highly unlikely that most Disclosurites would be willing to consider the possibility that they are being manipulated by the very people they believe they are finally triumphing over after a lifetime of lonely struggle![1]

The program has also given rise to the "discipline" known as *exopolitics*, whose proponents believe they are in ongoing, diplomatic communication with the aliens via an extraterrestrial organization or organizations somewhat on the order of the United Federation of Planets from the Star Trek mythology. In this they are imitating what they believe the Federal Government is capable of; according to them, the Feds don't have the monopoly on extraterrestrial contact, by golly! They too have made an alliance with the Powers of the Beyond. This leads us to ask how this "communication" with the aliens might be accomplished. Are their "allies" from the intelligence community feeding them all the latest diplomatic communiqués? Or are they in direct contact with the demons themselves through channeling and mediumship?

This second possibility is far from unlikely, given that the well-known psychic researcher Andrija Puharich, asso-

[1] From a correspondent: "Bill Cooper saw classified gov[ernment] doc[ument]s on aliens which he said were planted to generate 'insider' accounts for 'disclosure.' These 'secret' doc[ument]s were circulated to officers with 'access' to create leaks from 'insiders.'"

ciate of Aldous Huxley and the man who introduced Uri Geller to American audiences, consultant to the Pentagon on the military uses of parapsychology, participant in the MK-ULTRA mind-control experiments conducted by the CIA, was also involved, along with a group of eight colleagues that included members of some of America's first families, in channeling (through an East Indian medium) a group of "extraterrestrial entities" known as *The Nine*. The story is recounted in Peter Levenda's book of the same name, which we have referred to several times already.

This project would appear to be the ancestor of various later New Age alien channelings, such as *The Pleiadian Agenda* by Barbara Hand Clow (1995). Furthermore, when I contacted the Exopolitics Institute in Hawaii, founded by Dr. Michael Salla, who once received a Ford Foundation grant and who has a history of connection with the Center for Global Peace at the American University in DC, I made some very interesting discoveries. Impersonating a UFO true believer I asked the man who answered the phone if they were in touch with extraterrestrial organizations representing a consortium of planets, something like the Intergalactic Council the hippies believed in, and he said "yes." Then I asked him if two-way communication was ongoing between the Institute and the extraterrestrials; again he said "yes." And when I asked him by what means, he answered, "telepathy."[2]

---

[2] From a correspondent: "An expolitics leader claims on mass media to have encountered Jesus Christ. There is the religious angle, roping Christians into UFO belief. Why, Jesus confirms exopolitics!"

✳

To sum up, the "outer" explanation of the UFO phenomenon and the human activities surrounding it is as follows: The phenomenon is real, and largely inexplicable according to conventional science, though theories abound. In view of this, national governments, or cabals within them, or various extra-governmental power blocs, have said to themselves: "If we can't explain or control the UFO phenomenon, we can at least use it to our benefit." Consequently they spread the belief that national governments know a great deal about the phenomenon and what's behind it, and that such governments are in fact in ongoing contact with intelligent extraterrestrial beings, but must officially deny this for obvious reasons.

In other words, the actual disinformation being disseminated is not in service of the alleged Massive Government Coverup, which in practical terms would be almost impossible to pull off, but rather a highly successful attempt by some group or groups to make the population *believe* that a Massive Government Coverup exists, that the government wishes above all things to debunk the UFO phenomenon—a much easier task. (This is not to say that the military and intelligence community do not possess great masses of classified data on UFOs and alien contact, simply that they do not necessarily understand what they are or why they are appearing; this, at least, is Jacques Vallee's belief.) The effect of this affirmation/denial technique in terms of the more "exoteric" aspects of social engineering is fivefold:

(1) It protects the national governments from being called

upon to actually produce the alien diplomats they are supposedly in contact with.

(2) It lends such governments an aura of preternatural power, and terror, since they appear to have as allies highly "advanced" beings, beings from Beyond, who certainly do not rule by the will of the people.

(3) The practice of openly denying while covertly affirming the existence of extraterrestrials is an example of two mind-control techniques. The first, detailed above, is the one I call "subliminal contradiction": contradictory bits of information are proposed to the human mind as equally true, and the contradiction between them carefully kept from rising into consciousness; this technique stuns the critical faculties and puts the mind of the individual or collective subjected to it into a highly suggestible state. The second technique, which I call "deferred closure," by continually promising to satisfy and at the same time continually frustrating the innate need and function of the human mind to come to a consistent view of reality, produces a state of "closure-starvation," after which almost any belief that promises to provide the desperately needed closure will be seized upon as true and believed implicitly like a straw clutched by a drowning man. It will be believed because it is seen, not as an alien notion being imposed upon the subject against his will, but as the product of his own creativity, insight, perseverance, and self-sacrifice.

(4) It makes the true UFO believers feel as if they are part of a growing and increasingly successful campaign to force

the hand of the U.S. government, that they are both persecuted martyrs and victorious heroes. This is a perfect example of the *government co-optation* of *anti-government action*, the creation of a "controlled opposition," a method of social engineering that is certainly not limited to the UFO field.

(5) By fostering the mass belief in alien contact, it acts to break down traditional paradigms of reality, including religious worldviews, in order to make the imposition of a One World Government, and possibly a One World Religion, easier to swallow—a religion that must appear to any well-informed believer of the Abrahamic religions as the regime of Antichrist. As General Douglas MacArthur (who happened to be a Freemason) said on Sept. 2, 1945 (recounted by Peter Levenda in *A Warm Gun*, the second book in his *Sinister Forces* trilogy):

> We have had our last chance. If we cannot devise some more equitable system, our Armageddon will be at our door. *The problem basically is theological* and involves a spiritual recrudescence, an improvement of human character that will synchronize with our most matchless advances in science, art, literature, and all the material and cultural developments of the past two thousand years. It must be of the spirit if we are to save the flesh [emphasis mine].

It is possible to see this as a call for a Christian revival in Western civilization. The general, however, does not appeal here to Christian tradition, but to science, literature, and art. His pronouncement is also a succinct statement of the basic premises of both *The Day the Earth Stood Still*, whose theme is in no way Christian, and *Red*

Planet Mars, whose premise pretends to be Christian but is in fact materialist and atheistic; it almost fits him to be considered one of the ideological founders, the "grand old men," of the New Age Movement!

Furthermore, as I have already pointed out, the human activities surrounding the UFO phenomenon have an "inner" or "esoteric" explanation as well: that certain individuals and groups within national governments and/or the intelligence community and/or various extra-governmental power blocs actually *are* in touch with "extraterrestrial intelligences," but in a much different way than they wish the public to believe. These "intelligences" are demons, and those in touch with them, black magicians. What to the "exoteric" social engineers are activities of deception designed to alter mass belief, to the "esoteric" magicians, the "metaphysicists," are acts of demonic invocation: the mass *belief* in extraterrestrials, and the mass *suggestion* programs that foster this belief, actually aid these *awliya al-Shaytan* in their attempt to contact those entities and to release their baleful influence upon an unsuspecting world.

The esoteric dimension of the UFO phenomenon and the human activities surrounding it also manifests (as we have touched on before) in terms of an inverted metaphysics. To reiterate: just as subliminal contradiction is the satanic shadow of the Absolute, so deferred closure is the satanic shadow of the metaphysical principle, enunciated by metaphysician Frithjof Schuon (who was in some ways a "successor" to René Guénon) that God, as Absolute Reality, is necessarily also Infinite Possibility—which is why Scripture informs us that "with God all things are

167

possible" [Matthew 19:26]. If the intuitive sense of Infinite Possibility becomes alienated from the intuitive sense of Absolute Reality, the Absolute will falsely appear, not as the inviolable source of all stability, security, and certainty, but rather as a kind of "Absolutist" Divine Tyrant. At the same time, our perception of the Divine Infinity will be transformed from a vision of Infinite Life into an endless pursuit of an elusive wholeness that always escapes our grasp, one that leads only to the dissipation, and ultimately the destruction, of the soul that attempts it, or is lured into it. It is this deluded quest that led William Blake to say, "More! More! is the cry of a mistaken soul; less than All can never satisfy man." If subliminal contradiction is the satanic inversion of the Absolute, and consequently of the Masculine aspect of the Divinity, deferred closure is *avidya-maya*, the satanic inversion of the Divine Feminine. Subliminal contradiction stuns and oppresses us with a heavy hand; deferred closure teases us, drains our vitality, until we become its slaves, its eunuchs.

One final and highly interesting piece of the UFO puzzle may have been provided by a strange figure known as Prophet Yahweh—a black man who dresses a bit like a Muslim and who claims to be able to summon UFOs at will. In a 2008 news editorial on ABC Channel 13 in Las Vegas, Nevada,[3] he was shown as apparently able to induce a swift, high-flying orange sphere to materialize on command, which was filmed by the startled news crew. Prophet Yahweh had issued a challenge to the media,

---

[3] This story was available on YouTube in 2011 or 2012 at http://www.youtube.com/watch?v=ObD_ujS0t9E.

claiming he possessed this ability; Channel 13 responded by naming the place, date, and time when the UFO was to appear, apparently hoping to produce an entertaining segment debunking an inflated but harmless crank. But when the UFO actually did appear, they were (apparently) non-plussed. It is possible, of course, that Channel 13 was in on the stunt. But if they weren't, a couple of other scenarios suggest themselves: either the Prophet was in radio contact with human agents able to produce the phenomenon at will, or he did in fact possess the psychic ability to invoke the apparition of UFOs. In other words, he was either a disinformation agent or an actual magician—possibly both (though he had more the demeanor of a victim, possibly a victim of mind-control, than of a powerful and self-confident Magus). Now, I remember when, as a child in the late 1950s, my family and I used to gather at night on our patio overlooking San Francisco Bay to view the Perseid meteor shower, which takes place in August. Gazing up at the starry sky for hours, my mind would wander to the subject of flying saucers. I had the distinct feeling that if I wished hard enough, I could make one appear— and I don't think I am alone in this fantasy, which seems to be one aspect of the "UFO archetype" in collective belief.

✶

In conclusion—leaving aside for now the possibility of organized demonic invocation to usher in the Antichrist, which not every reader will accept, to say the least—I believe that UFOs and alien contact are both very real phenomena and elements of a modern myth that has been partly created, and certainly widely manipulated, by various governmental and globalist forces for their own purposes. Until the UFO debunkers take the hard evidence for the reality of UFOs seriously, and the UFO believers do the same with the hard evidence that their conception of the manifestation is being manipulated by people who do not have their best interests at heart, no sort of scientific, or psychological, or political objectivity will be possible with regard to the UFO phenomenon and its profound effects upon the human race.

Addendum

It is important to realize that, among what used to be called "the educated classes," a belief in the reality of extraterrestrial life is not limited to a few scientists and a handful of psychiatrists. Monsignor Corrado Balducci (1923–2008), a Roman Catholic theologian of the Vatican Curia, long-time exorcist for the Archdiocese of Rome, and a Prelate of the Congregation for the Evangelization of Peoples and the Society for the Propagation of the Faith, became well-known in UFOlogist circles for his belief in extraterrestrial life. He is quoted as maintaining, on the one hand, that "As God's power is limitless, it is not only possible but also likely that inhabited planets exist" (in other words, that physically-embodied extraterrestrials are likely a reality), but also that

> It is probable that there are other beings . . . because there is too much discrepancy between human and angelic nature, of which we have the theological certainty. And since in man, the spirit is subordinate to matter, and since the Angels are alone spirit, it is probable that beings exist

with very much less body and matter than we have. They could be those that we call UFO [aliens], these persons that would appear with these wagons [i.e., vehicles] and that also have not only one science, but a natural ability to be our guardians.[4]

In this second quotation he is approaching the Greek notion of the *daimones* and the Muslim doctrine of the Jinn. He also maintains that extraterrestrial encounters "are not demonic, they are not due to psychological impairment, and they are not a case of entity attachment" (apparently a non-traditional Novus Ordo Catholic term, derived from Spiritualism, denoting demonic possession). At this point, Monsignor Balducci exhibits the effects of both an incomplete cosmology and a lack of "discernment of spirits." Anyone who has read Dr. John Mack's book *Abduction*, and who also both believes in demons and understands their nature, will be forced to conclude that the majority of the terrifying encounters he reports have to do with the demonic, and nothing else. Many of these encounters appear to be cases of vexation (physical attack) or obsession (mental attack) rather than full possession. And yet the fact that, as Dr. Mack informs us, many of the "entities" who end by abducting their adult victims began as "imaginary playmates" during the victims' childhoods, is evidence that demonic possession is also a distinct possibility in some cases, as least insofar as we can define "familiar spirits" as "possessing" demons, not merely "obsessing" ones. If this exorcist for the Archdiocese of Rome had been

---

[4] From Monsignor Balducci's Wikipedia article, accessed 2011 or 2012; see his present article at http://www.youtube.com/watch?v=ObD_ ujSot 9E.

able to survey thoroughly and dispassionately his Church's archives relating to demonic activity, he would have seen that his description of the UFO aliens as possessing a kind of semi-material body, subtler than the human but grosser than the angelic, can certainly be applied to demons; as Fr Malachi Martin (himself an exorcist) points out in *Hostage to the Devil*, demons are often associated with specific localities in the physical world, as angels never are. It is possible that Msgr. Balducci shied away at this point from allowing that the UFO aliens (or some of them) might be demons, because he encountered certain manifestations that seemed generally benevolent, or at least neutral; at this crossroads he might have profited from the Muslim doctrine that "some of the Jinn are Muslim and some are *kafirun* (unbelievers)," the unbelieving Jinn being precisely demons, *shayatin*. Furthermore, to maintain that any subtle but not fully spiritual being can be a *guardian* to humanity is a strictly pagan belief; according to traditional Catholic doctrine, our guardians are necessarily *angels*, not *daimones*.

That a high-ranking Catholic exorcist was apparently unable to tell the difference between a guardian angel and a familiar spirit is one more glaring indication of the tragedy of the Novus Ordo Church since the Second Vatican Council. It is possible that, due to the weakening of the theurgic powers of the Novus Ordo stemming from the virtual deconstruction of the sacramental order, certain Catholic exorcists who came into intimate contact with demons, not realizing that they now lacked the spiritual potency that would protect them from these beings, and also in view of the fact that Catholic doctrine has been rendered relatively vague and ambiguous since Vatican II, may have become deluded by them—if not actually possessed. This possibility is rendered all the more likely in light of the recent announcement by a chief exorcist of the Diocese of Rome, Fr Gabriele Amorth (d. 2016), that the new rites of exorcism are basically ineffective.

Part III

Alien Disclosure:
The Great Game, UFO Division

*

A Response to Michael Salla

Alien Disclosure:
The Great Game, UFO Division

[An updated response to Michael Salla's article "Is Tom DeLonge's To The Stars Academy a Deep State Operation?" on the Exopolitics website, July 11, 2018]

This article, written in 2018, will hopefully provide some further explanatory background to the abrupt about-face of the U.S. government, in 2021, from an official position that UFOs—now called UAPs or "unidentified aerial phenomena"—are either delusions or recognizable natural or humanly-produced happenings, to one that accepts the phenomenon as "real," presently inexplicable, and of serious concern to the government and the military. As I have already made abundantly clear, is my belief that this radical break with the past is merely one phase of a well-planned and long-term social engineering effort to plant a belief in UFO aliens in the collective mind, so as to shift the prevailing paradigm in the western world away from Christianity and Democracy toward Luciferian Technocracy, Transhumanism etc.

According to Wikipedia, "Thomas Matthew DeLonge, (born December 13, 1975) is an American musician, singer, songwriter, author, record producer, actor, and filmmaker. In 2015, DeLonge founded an entertainment company called To The Stars, Inc. which, in 2017 he merged into a larger To The Stars Academy of Arts & Sciences. Aside from the entertainment division, the new company has aerospace and science divisions dedicated to ufology and the fringe science proposals of To The Stars' co-founder, Harold Puthoff." Puthoff, along with Russel Targ, was among those who studied the psycho-physical powers of Uri Geller at the Stanford Research Institute—and Geller's name, as we have already seen, has been associated with parapsychologist Andrija Puharich (who wrote a biography of him), as well as—according to Peter Levenda—Lawrence Livermore Laboratory, fringe physicist Jack Sarfatti, and filmmaker Steven Spielberg.

FIRST LET ME REITERATE that I believe the UFO phenomenon to be real, that although it is inexplicable according to contemporary physics and consensus reality, it is nonetheless all-too-well "understood," and exploited, by sectors of the military and intelligence communities working in tandem with various trans-governmental power blocs. But rather than delving directly into the question of who these people are and what their central agenda might be—as I have already done above—I will limit myself here in Part III to trying to throw further light on some of the ways the UFO phenomenon is being manipulated for purposes of social engineering.

Since the 1950s, a central, operative idea in the UFO community has been "the government knows a lot about UFOs, but they won't tell." This belief led UFOlogists to lobby the government to reveal what it supposedly knows, an effort that in the end produced the Disclosure Movement. Next, figures from the military and intelligence communities (often of retirement age, since one common way spy agencies deal with superannuated spooks is to put them on "UFO duty") began to present themselves to the

Disclosure Movement as whistleblowers who had betrayed their employers or former employers at great risk to themselves, and had now gone over to the good guys in the name of "disinterested truth." Of course the Disclosure Movement people, who had felt marginalized for years and were usually dismissed as mere UFO nuts, ate up whatever the so-called whistleblowers told them. Vindication at last—*and by real government officials!*

Then people like me came along and spoiled everything for the Disclosurites by pointing out, as I did in my book *Vectors of the Counter-Initiation* (2012), the likelihood that these whistleblowers were actually Deep State infiltrators, and giving evidence to support this contention.

So now the Disclosurites, including some of the whistleblower/infiltrators themselves, have apparently been forced to admit the possibility that the Disclosure Movement may in fact be a Deep State creation designed to implant certain beliefs in the collective mind. And one obvious way, under these conditions, for any particular Deep State infiltrator (Michael Salla, for example) to keep his credibility with the Movement is for him to denounce other Disclosurites (Peter Levenda, for example) as agents of the Deep State, thus picturing himself as a sincere researcher, or whistleblower. (Are you with me?)

This is not to say that the information revealed by infiltrators who denounce other infiltrators is *all* disinformation; since it has to be credible to those Disclosurites who are becoming increasingly sophisticated in their analysis of mind-control and social engineering techniques, a lot of it will need to be true and perceptive. What could be more interesting and enlightening, for example, than a photo of

Tom DeLonge and Peter Levenda next to *John Podesta*, such as appeared on the Exopolitics Website in July of 2018 as part of the article "Is Tom DeLonge's To the Stars Academy a Deep State Operation?" by Michael Salla? Nonetheless, disinformation will still make up a healthy percentage the infiltrators' revelations, according to the technique of "tell nine truths so as to lend credibility to one lie." Next, the infiltrators who were denounced by other infiltrators will probably come forward to denounce their denouncers, planting more disinformation in the process thereby, as well as revealing more plausible facts and interesting theories to maintain their own credibility. We should *not* assume, however, that those who denounce or debunk each other couldn't in fact be working together.

The operative tactic here is to provide an endless stream of contradictory information so as to stun and exhaust the critical faculties of sincere investigators, thus rendering them disoriented and suggestible; this method has been part of the UFO disclosure/denial cycle all along, beginning with the official disclosure, followed immediately by the official denial, of the Roswell crash in 1947.

I have already explained how this particular technique ("unconscious contradiction" and "deferred closure") induces its victims to construct patterns in areas where no such patterns exist, first, in order to explain the UFO phenomenon itself, secondly, to try and make sense of the hidden agenda of the government and/or the "men in black" in their dealings with the Disclosurites. We are much more likely to believe an explanation that we have constructed ourselves with a great investment of time and energy than one we suspect might have been implanted in us by an outside force. This technique has the added advantage of giving the social engineers insight into the "collective unconscious" of the populace they want to influence. And if this approach doesn't live up to expectations in terms of its ability to implant beliefs in the collective mind, still, the technique of unconscious contradiction will be effective in controlling us by weakening both our hope that anything can be known for sure in the area of UFOlogy, as well as our belief that there is such thing as the real, objective truth "out there"—a strategy that might be called "induced nihilism" or "weaponized postmodernism."

In brief, the goal of unconscious contradiction is, first, to pressure legitimate researchers to call it quits, and second (but more ambitiously), to train whole populations either to stop asking questions, since there is no "real truth" to be known, or ask them in a self-defeating way.

As for deferred closure, the Disclosurites, having spent decades trying to force the government to come clean, and thinking themselves on the brink of final success when the whistleblowers appeared, must now contend with the deep disappointment they feel as they begin to realize that some of these apparently helpful whistleblowers might actually be infiltrators operating according to some hidden Deep State agenda. But, because success was *almost* in sight, most of the sincere Disclorurites will press forward with their investigations (which to their great frustration must now include paranoia-inducing investigations into the legitimacy of their own movement!) with a renewed vigor fueled by this very frustration. Unfortunately, due to their experience of the cycle of ever-intensifying hope and frustration over many years, if and when an *official admis-*

sion appears, containing the *official version* of who the aliens are, they will most likely accept it without question, and with triumph, relief, and gratitude, no matter how hopeless or outlandish it might appear. (Still with me?)

These two mind-control techniques, unconscious contradiction and deferred closure, are not unknown to contemporary psychology. Unconscious contradiction is a method of inducing an extreme form of *cognitive dissonance* in which an inconsistency between two beliefs, or between a belief and a related action, is not overcome by altering one of the terms, since this is perceived to be impossible, but is rather *frozen* at the point where the contradiction is first encountered. Deferred closure is a method of exploiting the universal psychological tendencies known as the need for *cognitive closure*—the inability to perpetually tolerate a failure to determine what is true—and *apophenia*—the need to form a consistent pattern, whether or not such a pattern is objectively justified, when confronted with cognitive or perceptual chaos.

The social engineers have apparently studied these principles and learned how to use them for the engineering of mass belief; and part of this agenda appears in the Michael Salla article. Since I blew the whistle on him as a likely Deep State infiltrator in *Vectors of the Counter-Initiation* (2012), apparently he is now trying to shift that stigma to others. Those who have read Salla's article may have noticed how, after mentioning the Deep State, he uses the unnecessary (and unnecessarily capitalized) term "Deep Space." *DEEP STATE?* DEEP SPACE. *DEEP SPACE?* DEEP STATE. This is probably done in order to set up a *subliminal identification*. If Deep State equals Deep Space, then its powers are effectively infinite. Drawing upon the old Gnostic meme of the evil Hiemarmene, the Fate Archon or Goddess of Destiny associated with astrological fatalism, we might characterize this subliminal identification as warning us, in effect: *Beware! The stars are watching you.* David Icke, the well-known investigator of the "Reptilians," whose often insightful "conspiracy theories" are compromised by his lack of belief in an objective metaphysical order based on Truth rather than deception, also makes a connection between Deep State and Deep Space. The final upshot of this identification is nothing less than the suggestion that *Satan rules the universe*, that *Lucifer is God.*

✳

The intelligence/social engineering community, having had about a century by now to perfect their skills, have gotten techniques like those just summarized down to an exact science. They have almost certainly studied Jungianism, world mythologies, neuro-linguistic programming, perceptual psychology, comparative theology, and traditional metaphysics, looking for "archetypes" or "innate ideas" they can use to manipulate the mass mind. If this is in fact the case, one of the secondary but increasingly important fruits of a serious study of comparative religion and traditional metaphysics will be the ability to *detect* deliberate inversions of theological doctrines and metaphysical principles for purposes of mass mind-control. (The best introductory book to this study is the one-volume encyclopedia *A Treasury of Traditional Wisdom*, edited by Whitall Perry.)

The Abyss has been looking into us for long enough. It is

time for us, after becoming as spiritually grounded and metaphysically well-informed as possible, to begin looking back into it, and so come to a deeper understanding of exactly what is being done to us—and maybe even who is doing it.

Update, June 2021:
The Engineered Stretching of Credulity

Now that the "reality" of UFO or UAP sightings has been "admitted" by the U.S. government and the Pentagon—a "revelation" that was perfectly prepared for by the collective shock and challenge to consensus reality represented by the global Covid-19 pandemic—I can foresee eight further levels of revelation, each one beginning as a period of hotly-contested speculation, only to ultimately take its place among accepted "facts," each new set of "facts" representing a new phase in a socially-engineered paradigm shift in the Western world from Christianity and democracy to transhumanism and Luciferian technocracy:

Revelation Two:

The supposed existence of recovered debris of alien spacecraft. Apparently To The Stars Academy already claims to be in possession of such debris, or else of materiel back-engineered from a crashed UFO. Their website also reveals (as of September, 2021) that they have signed a contract with the U.S. Army to provide them with this materiel. If private venture capitalists want to risk investing in technologies that may or may not exist, as they did in Elizabeth Holmes' Theranos Corporation, which could attract nearly one billion dollars in venture capital to market a non-existent blood testing device, that is their right. But the tax payers have an equal right to demand that TTSA produce concrete proof of the extraterrestrial origin of their product in the form of an actual crashed UFO, not simply rumors of one.

Revelation Three:
The reality of alien abduction.

Revelation Four:
The supposed reality of back-engineering of alien space-craft.

Revelation Five:
The supposed existence of recovered alien bodies.

Revelation Six:
The supposed or actual existence of contact between UFO aliens and officials of the government and the military.

Revelation Seven:
The supposed existence of ongoing diplomatic relations between governments and/or international institutions with alien representatives of "the Galactic Council" or some similar consortium of planets, including sharing of technology, stretching back for decades.

Revelation Eight:
The supposed existence of significant covert influence of space aliens on human society, psychology, and biology, including the reality and effect of alien implants and alien/human hybridization, stretching back for centuries or millennia, culminating in the declaration that these beings, through genetic engineering, actually created the human race.

Revelation Nine: The full admission of the *interdimensional* reality of space aliens, their transcendence of the limits of terrestrial space and time, whether or not this finally culminates in the triumphant admission that these beings are in fact those who were once superstitiously characterized as "demons" or "fallen angels" by a debunked and superseded Christianity.

A well-recognized brainwashing technique involves the alternation of terror with relief. After a period of torture, the sudden transformation of one's torturers into helpful friends will often be accepted with immense gratitude, no matter how implausible such a transformation might be when viewed objectively; the victim has been deliberately induced to mistake the feeling of relief for the warmth of friendship. (Those seriously involved in the struggle against the passions will recognize this as a common ploy of the demons of temptation, who are adept at changing back and forth with lightning speed from indulgent friends to pitiless accusers.) Furthermore, there are indications that the social engineers may have learned how to apply this technique on a mass scale. Whether or not the Covid-19 pandemic was deliberately created in order to transform global society for the "great reset" (as some have speculated), it was likely recognized that the collective shock to consensus reality represented by the pandemic was an ideal time to officially disclose the reality of UFOs. And if Covid could create the *shock of terror*, we must be vigilant against the *shock of relief* that could be generated by Covid's end. This second shock might provide the perfect opportunity for a staged advent of the Aliens as the wonderful, saving manifestation we had been waiting for all along, perhaps even the *material reality* behind the religious "myth" of the Second Coming of Christ!

It would be good for Christians to remember at this point that when Christ really does come back for the second time it will not be to solve earthly problems or fascinate us with the endless wonders of the material universe, but to fulfill a single predestined purpose: to judge the living and the dead. Likewise, Muslim readers should also remember that, according to the premier Muslim historian Ibn Khaldun as well as many other sources, the return of the Prophet Isa (Jesus) to slay *al-Dajjal* (Antichrist) before the coming of the Hour—Sayiddna Isa, who is considered to be an immortal prophet, like Ilyas (Elias) and Idris (Enoch)—has always been central to traditional Muslim eschatology. Are we now in the hour of his advent? We certainly could be, although this question is one that can only be answered definitively by the event itself. Until then, we should conscientiously heed the traditional advice that has always been given to both Christians and Muslims, though not always followed by them: to watch for the appearance of the Divine Command, and pray that we will have the discernment to recognize it and the courage to obey it, no matter what the cost.

Part IV

Reordering Primary UFO Beliefs:
A Review of the Argument

✳

Reordering Primary UFO Beliefs
A Review of the Argument

RATIONAL INQUIRY into the UFO phenomenon has
been hampered by certain unwarranted and largely unconscious associations, or conceptual couplings, between the
primary facts characterizing it. These unnecessary associations need to be broken and new and more illuminating
associations formed. If we are to accomplish this, however,
we will need to accept the fact that *rational* does not equal
materialistic. As is abundantly proved, for example, by
Roman Catholic scholastic philosophy, logic and rationality are not to be identified with the root assumptions of
materialism or scientism; logic can be applied to analyze
the implications even of divinely-revealed theological
principles, as well as to the "discernment of spirits" that
becomes necessary when we are confronted with paranormal phenomena, the possibility of demonic possession etc.
The following is one picture of how our common assumptions and conclusions regarding the UFO manifestation
might be fundamentally re-ordered.

Four Generally Accepted Facts
1) UFOs produce physical phenomena and leave physical
traces. 2) They affect the human psyche. 3) They produce
paranormal or psycho-physical phenomena—materializations, dematerializations, penetration of physical barriers

without altering them, etc. 4) There is good evidence for the existence of human deception activities surrounding the UFO phenomenon.

Three False Idea-Associations to be Uncoupled

PSYCHIC ≠ PSYCHOLOGICAL OR SUBJECTIVE

That UFOs affect the human psyche is well-established. This does NOT mean, however, that UFOs are the products of human psychological beliefs, delusions etc. The psychic effects of UFO encounters are not subjective impressions but are, according to all available evidence, objectively real.

PHYSICAL ≠ EXTRATERRESTRIAL

That UFOs produce physical manifestations and traces does not necessarily mean that they are spacecraft from other inhabited planets in the universe. Anyone conversant with the lore of the world of the paranormal, the known and recorded history of which lore covers several millennia, will know that the Psychic domain has always been considered capable of affecting the Physical, leaving physical traces and materializing physical objects, things that appear to exhibit all the characteristics of normal matter but which often dematerialize again after a short time—for example, the "angel hair" sometimes associated with UFO sightings. (The ontological domain of the Psychic is a separate world with its own characteristic potentialities and limitations, distinct from the Physical domain that lies "below" it on the ontological hierarchy or Great Chain of Being, and the

Spiritual domain that is situated "above" it.) Anyone who is well-informed as to the philosophy and phenomenology of the Psychic will immediately see that the UFO phenomenon conforms to the parameters of the Psychic or paranormal domain much more closely than to those of the Physical domain or the Spiritual domain. Astronauts like Yuri Gagarin or Neil Armstrong do not materialize and dematerialize before our eyes, walk through the walls of our bedrooms at night and hand us physical objects that later disappear into thin air; such phenomena are the stock in trade of another class of brings entirely. Furthermore, as premier UFOlogist Jacques Vallee points out, the UFO's and their occupants are unlikely to have made the interminable journey at the maddeningly sluggish speed of light through physical space from other inhabited planets because there are simply too many of them.

HUMAN DECEPTION ≠ COMPLETE HOAX— I.E., NO REAL UNEXPLAINED PHENOME- NON, WHETHER PSYCHIC OR PHYSICAL

Jacques Vallee, in *Messengers of Deception*, has presented documentary evidence for various human deception activities of the *Mission Impossible* variety clustering around the UFO phenomenon. However, the existence of such activities does *not* mean that UFOs are all a "hoax", a conclusion that is in no way supported by the available evidence. This begs the question: if these activities are not intended to make the population believe in the reality of UFOs when they are in fact unreal—by which I mean, easily explainable according to our normal assumptions about what reality is—then what is their purpose?

Three Examples of Ideas that might be Coupled or Associated in a Different Way

PSYCHIC = PARANORMAL

If, as I maintain, the UFO phenomenon closely fits the parameters of the paranormal or Psychic domain, then both the traditional lore and the modern research that deal with that domain, which Roman Catholicism names the "preternatural" and Islamic doctrine sees as the world of the Jinn, should take center stage in our attempts to make sense of UFOs. Physical measurements and research, and speculation based on them, will always have their place; however, we should place any Physical findings in the wider context of the Psychic rather than attempting to understand the Psychic according to the more limited parameters of the Physical.

PHYSICAL = PSYCHIC INTRUSIONS INTO PHYSICAL REALITY

Aerospace multi-millionaire Robert Bigelow, American's premier private-sector UFO researcher at this point in time (2021), is usually presented, as in the Netflix Original series *Top Secret UFO Projects: Declassified* (premiered August 2, 2021; 30% truth, 70% myth, speculation and propaganda), as believing that UFOs are extraterrestrial spacecraft. Yet he purchased (and then re-sold) Skinwalker Ranch in Utah, which has reportedly been host to every paranormal manifestation imaginable, including apparitions of Bigfoot (whose tracks, when followed, have been found to abruptly end in the middle of an open field), "classical" flying saucers, floating orbs, paranormally huge dogs, and (on one occasion) a six-foot-tall rabbit who stared motionlessly for many minutes at the people operating Skinwalker Ranch from outside their home. Are we to believe that the Sasquatches, the paranormal rabbits and dogs have all come here over thousands of light years from another inhabited planet? Clearly Bigelow is on the trail of something radically different than alien astronauts—an impression that is corroborated by the fact that one of his other research interests is the "scientific" inquiry into life after death.

Astrophysicist Travis Taylor, who did an extensive scientific investigation of the radical and nearly continuous paranormal activity at Skinwalker Ranch in Utah, which includes but is not limited to apparitions of UFOs, perfectly expressed, in a YouTube interview, the limitations of an approach to the paranormal based strictly on materialistic science when he said: "If you have something that can't be explained by modern physics as we know it, that means that there's more to physics than we know" [https://www.youtube.com/watch?v=uBabYbbhSgc&t=1s]. This is like saying that "If we encounter something in life that can't be explained by crystallography, that means that there's more to crystallography than we know"—whereas what it actually means is that there are many more ways and levels of knowing, and things to know, than crystallography can address. The same goes for physics. Physics is intrinsically limited to physical phenomena; it deliberately concentrates on this area to the exclusion of everything else; it is not designed to investigate non-physical realities.

If a modern scientist were confronted with a set of phenomena that could not presently be explained in materialistic terms, yet was aware of vast body of data that did claim to explain it according to the explicit principles of a non-materialistic science, would it be properly *scientific* of him or her to totally ignore that body of data, or at least to make no systematic study of it, relying instead only on vague rumors, anomalous reports taken out of context, and his or her own fragmentary and uninformed impressions? Obviously not. So when I assert that the true nature of what today we call "the paranormal" has *always been known*, at least in general terms, according to the canons of the non-materialistic science of traditional metaphysics, any serious and conscientious scientist must take what I say into account, or else stand convicted of a narrow-minded *scientistic* prejudice that has nothing truly scientific about it.

The traditional Catholics call the realm of the paranormal the "preternatural," as opposed to the supernatural, and have extensive records of certain aspects of its behavior, origin, and intentions. The Muslims understand this realm to be the world of the Jinn. The Sufis see it, or at least the proper center of it, as the *alam al-mithal*, the world of "image-exemplars." The Platonists call it the realm of the *daimones*, which lies between the plane of the gods or celestials, identifiable in some ways with the Universals or the Platonic Ideas, and the plane of the five senses. The shamans, the practitioners of what have sometimes been called the "animistic" religions, and others, have clearly-defined techniques for dealing with this world, protecting humanity from it and putting some of its powers to use. All this data is now available to any serious researcher, therefore any researcher who continues to ignore it may be suspected of not being serious. This is not to say that modern science has no contribution of its own to make to the study of the paranormal; far from it. The discovery by Travis Taylor and others that paranormal manifestations can be accompanied by bursts of microwaves or gamma waves, to take only one example, is of the greatest significance since it represents an approach to the study of preternatural phenomena that was not available to the ancients or to various primal peoples of today. Such studies have an important place in the work of producing a comprehensive theory of the paranormal. I believe that they will always be limited, however, to a study of the effects or reverberations of various *intrusions* of the paranormal into material reality. When it comes to a study of the non-material or subtle-material realm of the *daimones* as it is in itself, the proper approach cannot be through physics or any other materialistic science—any more than the areas of astronomy or biology can be *directly and comprehensively* studied through the science of crystallography. The tools of research must be proper to the body of data being studied.

HUMAN DECEPTIONS = ATTEMPTS TO PROFIT FROM THE UFO PHEMOMENON, NOT SIMPLY TO PROMOTE OR DEBUNK THE BELIEF IN IT

The following tentative conclusions are clearly speculative; they have not yet assumed the status of the four *facts* listed above. Nonetheless I believe that they represent the only theory to date that fully incorporates and explains these facts. The ability to demonstrate the possible relationships between sets of data whose causal connections had not previously been apparent, to present a pattern that incorporates all of them in single "elegant" design, is not in itself proof that the theory that allows us to do this is true. It does, however, constitute a convincing argument that the theory in question must be taken seriously.

One of the abiding themes in the traditional lore of the paranormal is that human beings can have interactions with the Psychic domain, either accidentally or deliberately; conscious and purposeful transactions between human beings and the Psychic are well represented in the traditional lore of shamanism, ceremonial magic etc. This contention is also abundantly demonstrated by modern science-based psychical research, such as that presented in *The End of Materialism* by Dr. Charles Tart, as well as by programs like the remote viewing experiments conducted by the CIA. In view of this, I would speculate that the human deception activities that routinely turn up in association with the UFO phenomenon—as, for example, the accurate prediction of "retired NORAD officer" Stanley A. Fulham, detailed above in Part II, that UFOs would appear in the skies above earth's cities on October 13, 2010, which they did—may represent attempts by human agents—perhaps according to the methodology of sympathetic or imitative magic—to attract the attention of various paranormal forces or beings, possibly in order to conclude ongoing alliances with them, as is apparently claimed by Dr. Michael Salla, director of the Exopolitics Institute. Less outlandish and more believable is that such deceptions could represent a concerted social engineering program designed to introduce a belief in all-powerful "aliens" into the collective psyche of humanity. In any case, Robert Bigelow, in a video interview, describes what seems to be at least the beginning of such a human/alien pact when he reports that a mass of floating orbs that appeared at Skinwalker Ranch would move at one point in response to human commands phoned in from miles away; likewise various individuals, such as the Prophet Yahweh mentioned above, seemingly possess the power to summon UFOs at will. The pagan invocations of aerospace pioneer Jack Parsons suggest a similar pact, either real or delusional, between human beings and paranormal powers. Thus we may legitimately speculate either that Bigelow and his peers have actually made a pact with the Powers of the Air, *or* that they believe they have, *or* that they would like to make the rest of us believe they have— if not now, then at some point in the future. The goal of this agenda, whether or not we accept the full reality of the treaty or pact in question, could be to shift the collective worldview of global society away from the traditional revealed religions, originating in the Spiritual domain, as well as from various established forms of governance, whether democratic or traditional, and toward belief in the paranormal, magical scientism, transhumanist technocracy etc.—a revolution that is obviously well under way already. If this is the case, there are undoubtedly many powerful groups and individuals now operating in today's world who believe—with good reason—that they could profit mightily from such a paradigm shift.

Part V

The Netflix Original Series,
Top Secret UFO Projects:
Declassified—

Historical / Scientific
Documentary
or
Religious Tract?

✳

The Netflix Original Series
Top Secret UFO Projects: Declassified—
Historical/Scientific Documentary or Religious Tract?

Top Secret UFO Projects: Declassified, which premiered in August of 2021—after which it was reviewed *Newsweek* and generated a stream of news stories on the internet—is a thinly-disguised and thoroughly-articulated social engineering gambit presented as a factual documentary. Since it essentially announces the advent of a new religion, one which proposes that we worship the "aliens," whether extraterrestrial or interdimensional, in the place of God— a religion whose prophets are CIA agents, military brass, and aerospace multimillionaires—at the very least it ought to succeed in calling into question the myth that the U.S. government has been trying to *debunk* the popular belief in UFOs for the past 70 years rather than covertly promoting it. Evidence for this covert promotion appears in *Top Secret UFO Projects: Declassified* when it asserts that whistleblowers who reveal what the government knows about the UFO phenomenon do so at risk of their lives, while at the same time presenting us with the findings of so-called whistleblowers like Colonel Philip J. Corso, Bob Lazar, Emery Smith and astronaut Edgar Mitchell, who have been operating freely for years, speaking, writing and appearing in videos, apparently with no negative consequences; two of them are interviewed in the documentary itself.

This hidden promotion of the UFO belief, which has now come to light in the present documentary and similar productions, has obviously been accompanied by a much more visible debunking campaign, one that has served to distract attention from the underlying pro-UFO agenda as well as to actively promote the *particular spin* on the popular belief in UFOs that certain forces wish to legitimize and employ, while cultivating this perspective more gradually and securely than an abrupt Disclosure would allow. Perhaps the idea has been to delay Disclosure until such time as the traditional religious worldview was weakened to the point where most believers would no longer possess the necessary criteria to correctly evaluate it. This slow-but-sure approach to social engineering is more-or-less in line with the gradualist method pioneered by the Fabian Socialists, which has largely been adopted by the Cultural Marxists as well.

Top Secret UFO Projects: Declassified is shot through with contradictory claims, often by the same experts and/or commentators—statements that are so diametrically opposed to each other that only someone who is half asleep, mesmerized, or suffering from Attention Deficit Disorder (as most of us seem to be nowadays, in one way or another) could fail to notice them. There is little chance that these mutually-exclusive statements could simply be accidental, based on poor writing or shoddy editing, or simply representative of different points-of-view. I suppose it's remotely possible that those who wrote and produced *Top Secret UFO Projects: Declassified* were simply not paying attention, but it seems much more likely that these glaring contradictions are deliberate and purposeful—which is strange, since those who wish to be believed are usually careful to make their arguments as consistent as possible. The present analysis will highlight these inconsistencies, as well as pointing out various statements that appear to reveal the underlying agenda on which the documentary is based.

Episode One, "Project Bluebook Unknown," is the least problematic. It is a well-researched history of the UFO phenomenon in the United States, and the human response to it, since World War II, in which the ideological drive of the series as a whole is not yet apparent; nonetheless it contains the first of the highly suspect accounts on which the growth of the UFO myth in the 20th century was based. According to this "likely story," researcher Rob Mercer, in response to a classified advertisement, took possession of a cache of documents stored in the garage of a former employee of Wright-Patterson Airbase, which supposedly contained all the UFO accounts that had been collected by, but later excluded from, Project Bluebook; the "documentary" then goes on to accept the validity of this leaked material with absolutely no corroborating evidence, and to use it as the basis for further arguments and speculations. Maybe this *is* actually a common way for the military to dispose of classified documents that are taking up too much office space… on the other hand, what we might be seeing here is an example of the double game that I believe the military and the intelligence community have been playing for many years, right up to the release of the Pentagon Report to Congress in 2021: the game of officially denying the reality of the UFO phenomenon while covertly spreading the belief in UFOs throughout the populace.

Episode Two, "The White House Cover-up," introduces us to the supposed existence of a top secret monitoring group within the CIA known as Majestic or MJ-12, who were supposedly tasked with concealing the truth about UFOs. Many things are claimed for this group; it is even asserted that one of the main reasons for the creation of the CIA itself was to conduct "covert operations" to study flying saucers. Only later do we find out that the first report of the existence of Majestic came in the form of a package anonymously placed in the mailbox of TV producer Jaime Shandera, containing a roll of film with microfiche photos of documents supposedly revealing the existence of MJ-12. More anonymously leaked documents relating to Majestic and other supposedly covert projects turned up over the years. The "contentious" nature of these leaked files is admitted by UFO writer Richard Dolan, then quickly ignored; from then on they are simply taken as fact. These documents might be legitimate; they might be false; they might be a little of both—but for a supposedly factual documentary to largely accept, without independent corroboration, evidence that would be thrown out of any court makes it clear that we are viewing a polemic, not a documentary. UFO researcher J.J. Hurtak shows us a memo from the Majestic documents supposedly signed by Harry Truman; he tells us the signature is "consistent with other government papers that show on the highest levels" (Show what? Levels of what?) while pointing his finger to the sky to a quick shot of a hovering UFO. Then premier British UFO spokesperson Nick Pope makes his appearance to tell us of a document he apparently once saw, recounting a meeting between Winston Churchill and Eisenhower during the war where they had decided that UFOs were real but that this shouldn't be revealed during wartime because it might "destroy the Church." The source of the document was said to be a story told to a British scientist by his grandfather, who was supposedly one of Churchill's body guards during the meeting in question. (Hard evidence: case closed.)

Next Travis Walton appears, who tells the harrowing story of his famous UFO abduction in Arizona in 1975. One revealing facet of this fascinating account is the strange evaluation, reminiscent of the "Stockholm Syndrome," that Walton gives of the true intent of his tormentors, whose unasked-for intervention was deeply traumatizing to him on a permanent basis. He says: "I screamed at them, yelled all sorts of things. . . . I think just the entire circumstances of whatever was done with me and to me sort of sends a message about their real intentions that took me years to realize, that they weren't just collecting humans in order to dissect them . . . or maybe eat them . . . they were most likely intervening in what happened to me to correct a severe extreme damage that was caused by a burst of energy that was probably accidental." This, however, seems to be pure conjecture, besides contradicting innumerable other accounts of alien abductions that were in no way in helpful response to perceived injuries and obviously had nothing accidental about them—as, for example, the nightmarish abduction experience of Terry Lovelace, a medic at Whiteman Air Force Base, and his friend Toby during a hiking trip through Devil's Den State Park in Arkansas, which is recounted immediately after Walton's. Lovelace tells of the night when they saw a huge triangular UFO passing overhead. He fell into a stupor and later awakened to find himself and his friend surrounded by a ring of diminutive ET's, whom he initially took to be children. But his companion set him straight: "Terry, man" said Toby, "those ain't no little kids. Don't you remember? They took us and they hurt us." "And then," Lovelace tells us, "I had flashes of memory, and he was right: they did take us and they did hurt us." Here the damage is certainly not accidental, while the aliens' actions clearly have nothing to do with healing accidental injuries. To the degree that Walton feels compelled to interpret traumatic abuse as helpful and benevolent, we must suspect that he is not yet fully in possession of his faculties. He goes on to say: "I do not believe aliens are bad. I believe that extremely advanced technologies (and) civilizations evolve out of what we call evil. . . ." No line of reasoning is given to support this conclusion, which certainly does not seem to be bourn out by Walton's own experience. It is also noteworthy that he uses the phrase "advanced technologies (and) civilizations evolve . . . out of evil." Apparently he means to say that they evolve "beyond" evil, yet his actual phraseology is suggestive of much deeper misgivings than he is apparently willing to admit. The technique of presenting something as positive and helpful while at the same time making it an object of terror, without in any way admitting the radical contradiction between these two propositions, serves to create *unconscious fear*, which is much more useful as a control technique than conscious terror. A soldier going into combat who knows he may die in an hour can martial all his forces to stand or fall; a person who is terrorized and at the same time given a way to view the thing terrorizing him as benevolent and protective has no way to do this. And note the telling phrase "what we *call* evil"—as if evil were no more than a socially-conditioned prejudice, rather than a sober fact that we trivialize at our supreme peril.

Next President Ronald Reagan is shown delivering an address to the UN in 1984, in which he makes the claim that the differences between nations would vanish if we were facing "an alien threat from outside this world," echoing a similar statement made by Douglas MacArthur at West Point in 1962; clearly this idea, which was commented on by Jacques Vallee in *Messengers of Deception* (1979), has been around for quite a while.

Episode Two floats the idea that UFO research, as well as the ultimate *political* authority in the United States, is now passing, or has already passed, from the public to the private sector, as witness aerospace CEO Robert Bigelow and rock star Tom DeLonge, founder of the To The Stars Academy; and of course Jeff Bezos and Elon Musk also come to mind in this context. According to Richard Dolan, leaving the ultimate authority for UFO research to the President of the United States, a mere democratically-elected official, would be "dangerous"; and Dolan ends the episode by saying that we should first pay attention to the *information* available about UFOs, not the *sources* of the information—to the spectacle itself, that is, and not to those who may be designing and controlling that spectacle. Needless to say, I have taken the opposite approach.

Episode Three, "Code Name Aurora," begins with the question: "Could the U.S. military's desire to reverse-engineer UFO technology for its own ends be behind its continuing reticence to disclose information about its UFO monitoring program?" This, however, is not the first question that needs to be asked and answered. The first question is: Has the U.S. military recovered or been provided with any UFO technology? Answer: We don't know. And the second question is: Do we know for sure whether or not the U.S. military has a desire, or a program, to reverse-engineer UFO technology? Answer: No. In any case, no documentary that uses leading questions based on rumor and hearsay to suggest facts that have in no way been established can be trusted as a serious analysis.

Next we are treated to the highly entertaining story recounted by Colonel Philip J. Corso of Fort Bliss Army Base, Arkansas, the author of *The Day After Roswell,* of an incident that took place in 1947 when he was a major at Ft. Riley Kansas. Apparently a "special cargo" had been secretly delivered that day, and Corso, being a naturally curious sort, figured that he'd poke around in it to see what he could turn up, so he chose one of the crates at random, pried it open, and what should he discover inside but an alien corpse! The corpse was not kept in a hermetically-sealed temperature-controlled coffin, just a regular wooden shipping crate. Imagine his surprise! Then the sergeant on duty turned up, at which point Corso told him, "really, Sarge, you could get in trouble being with me while

I'm messing around with a secret shipment like this, which I get to do because I'm duty officer; let's just back out of here are pretend that nothing happened. " (Seriously, these guys must imagine that we're *all* brain-dead, not just most of us.) Later Corso, now a colonel, was stationed at the White House. No Men In Black with threats of dire consequences should he reveal what he saw, just professional advancement and a prestigious job. In 1961 he supposedly received a file reporting on an alien autopsy that *he himself had supposedly witnessed* at Fr. Riley in 1947, as well as on alien technology recovered from the Roswell crash. According to Australian UFO researcher Mary Rodwell, Corso's job while at the White House included receiving alien technological gizmos and then turning them over to private corporations. And apparently he was also informed that our beloved Teflon was another gift from the aliens!

Next, former USAF scientist and medical researcher Emory Smith tells us that he isn't sure *exactly when* the reverse-engineering of alien technology began, only that—according to his researches in the Vatican archives, which contain *examples of such technology*—it has been going on since ancient times. Will the Vatican eventually advance its anti-Catholic ideology by publicly making this claim? Suffice it to say that the revelation of the reality of UFOs could not destroy the flimsy remaining shell of the Catholic Church, as Eisenhower and Churchill reportedly worried, if the Church itself backs this assertion, and even claims to have known all about it for centuries.

Then David Adair appears with his claim that he had developed an electromagnetic fusion containment engine by 1971, when he was taken to Area 51 to meet with General Curtis LeMay and shown an engine recovered from a UFO, similar in principle but immensely larger. Since the rest of the world, as of 2021, is spending billions of dollars to produce a workable fusion power source, Adair should really make his invention widely available for the good of humanity. He must have patented it, which means that it could make him a billionaire over night. The strange thing is that all the other fusion researchers in the world apparently neglected to seek and discover that patent. Oh, well; better late than never. I urge every reader of this review to appeal to Adair to make his technology known to everyone; we should all really *get after* him to do this—or else to demonstrate why he won't or can't; the future of humanity could depend on it. (I will give the subject of this paragraph a full "GB" rating, which stands for "*GIMME A BREAK*"! Be on the lookout for more paragraphs labeled "GB" below.)

Now we discover that Ben Rich, past director of the famous Skunk Works that developed the U-2 and SR-71 Blackbird spy planes, lectured to the UCLA School of Engineering in 1993; the last slide of the accompanying presentation reportedly showed a black disc leaving the earth's atmosphere, about which Rich commented, "we now have the technology to take ET home." When questioned by a student after the lecture about the propulsion of the craft, he was apparently told that it was based on ESP! (Why not?)

The episode ends with the story of CIA anti-terrorist specialist Luis Elizondo, who was tapped for UFO duty by a military monitoring group, then quit military service to join the To The Stars Academy in the private sector. He claims that the government possesses many samples of material from crashed UFOs, and that To The Stars has partnered with them to study it. Elizondo says that UFO propulsion is based on two factors, "nuclear" and "water", which are not directly related but which are nonetheless somehow related (whatever that means; earlier it was claimed to be based on "element 115"), and that—as should be obvious to all—we are already in the midst of Disclosure as we speak.

The true identity and intentions of Luis Elizondo remain unclear, and call for further research. Elizondo's Wikipedia article says:

> Luis Elizondo is a former U.S. Army Counterintelligence Special Agent and former employee of the Office of the Under Secretary of Defense for Intelligence. After his resignation in 2017, he joined the company To The Stars as its Director of Global Security and Special Programs. Elizondo left the company in late 2020 [*but was with To The Stars Academy in Sept. 2021*]. . . . Elizondo is the former director of the now defunct Advanced Aerospace Threat Identification Program. . . . According to the Department of Defense, the AATIP program was ended in 2012 after five years. Elizondo has said he worked with officials from the U.S. Navy and the CIA out of his Pentagon office for this program until October 2017, when he resigned to protest what he characterized as "excessive secrecy and internal opposition."

So we know that Luis Elizondo has an extensive background in the U.S. Intelligence community. Now, however, he is apparently at odds with his former employers and willing to make his intelligence expertise available to "the People" through his connection with the Disclosure Movement. However, since the military itself has now openly embraced elements of Disclosure in the June 2021 Pentagon Report to Congress, which has admitted (at the very least) that UFOs are real and inexplicable, it is entirely possible that Elizondo, far from being a renegade in flight from the intelligence community, is actually a loyal agent of their ongoing agenda.

On two occasions during my checkered career I was approached by individuals claiming to be ex-CIA agents or operatives who had quit the Agency and gone over to the "good guys" (me). I see this as a common ploy by the Firm to recruit "useful idiots", using as bait the possibility that the fished-for individual might become privy to "real CIA secrets" while still heroically tilting at the windmills of the Powers That Be. And it is well-known that the Disclosure Movement is full of "whistleblowers" with a military or intelligence background, who are routinely accepted as sincerely repentant villains who have seen the error of their ways and only here to help. In my opinion, however, it is much more likely that these individuals are still on the government dole, drawing their pay as infiltrators, spies and disseminators of the well-designed information, or quasi-information, that their employers want the Movement, and ultimately the general public, to accept.

In **Episode Four,** "Hacked and Leaked," the following contradictory account is offered regarding the release of information about the "tic-tac" and "gimbal" UFOs that figured in the now-famous Nimitz (aircraft carrier) encounters off San Diego in 2004:

NARRATOR: By releasing unclassified U.S. government reports in 2018 . . . journalist George Knapp changed the game...

KNAPP: I produced a document that was leaked from the government (?) . . . this information was never meant to be released to the public. The military did this behind the scenes in a classified program...

The narrator says that the documents were unclassified and Knapp claims that they were classified. Who should we believe?

Next, much more interestingly, Richard Dolan offers a very accurate and incisive piece of analysis:

The U.S. is great at making up false news stories and spreading them throughout the world—I mean, the CIA is a master of this, they have done this for decades. They are very good also at using the media to scare the public to engage in certain actions, they do this all the time. So they certainly would be able to do this about UFOs or UAPs. Like they have the capability to, if they were to release information, they could do it in such a way as to maximize fear to whatever level they want that would be useful to them.

Truer words were never spoken. My question is, if the CIA is a master of the false story, then *why does Dolan trust Luis Elizondo*, with his past military intelligence and CIA connections? Is it entirely beyond the realm of possibility that Dolan's analysis might perfectly describe Elizondo's methodology and intentions? Beyond that, it is it not also possible that the above statement by Dolan also perfectly describes the methodology and intentions of *Top Secret UFO Projects: Declassified* itself? Here we enter the field of the gambit that revisionist historian Michael Hoffman calls the Revelation of the Method, according to which the clandestine social engineers will sometimes suddenly and openly reveal exactly what they've been up to. Why would they do this? After a long history of marginalizing and persecuting whistleblowers, why would they blow the whistle on themselves? For two reasons. First, the act of self-whistleblowing works to co-opt and neutralize the true whistleblowers, take the wind out of their sails. If Cassandra's accusers suddenly turn around and tell her, "Chill out, Cassie, we've known this all along," she immediately loses all her relevance. Secondly, for the perpetrators to blow the whistle on themselves transforms them from liars who must be exposed into honest men and women who have admitted the truth about themselves and so should be believed, thereby employing (on an entirely unconscious level) the martial arts principle of turning the attacker's strength against him. "If they openly describe this method of news-control they *couldn't* be using it themselves" we naively conclude. Those who fall for this ploy have forgotten to ask one simple question: If a liar admits he's lying while still continuing to lie, does that make him an honest man?

Episode Five, "Soviet Secrets," tells us that "Some interested parties in the United States . . . were afraid that the Soviet Union may use the UFO frenzy in the United States to cause some kind of a mass hysteria, and they were also actively thinking about using the UFO phenomenon as a means to do psychological warfare in the Soviet Union." We must consider the possibility, however, that these "interested parties" may presently be using the UFO phenomenon to do psychological warfare against the American people, a much easier target and likely a much more rewarding one for the social engineers who are doing their best to manage and manipulate virtually every aspect of our lives. And the best way to hide such manipulation would be to convince the people, against all evidence to the contrary, that their response to the covert social engineering directives they are being subjected to is actually a product of their own collective self-determination. The ideal way to manage such a regime would be to utilize the "soft power" of information rather than overt police state tactics. This has been the preferred mode of governance in the United States since World War Two, with the police and the military always waiting in the wings to be called upon if and when the softer approach fails—which it often has, and likely will in the future. J.J. Hurtak tells us:

> Let us look beyond the politics of the old regime . . . when younger people begin to expand their consciousness and see the bigger picture, then government authority will be, shall we say, secondary; teaching authority, or the social sciences, will be primary. We will have a worldwide internet of information that will download information quickly so everyone in the world will be a citizen diplomat, we'll have the opportunity to have contact without going to a military source. . . .

If "contact" means "alien contact," which is certainly implied, the plan seems to be to set up data-bases and audio-visual feeds available to everyone, where not only masses of data on the UFO phenomenon are easily accessible but also direct channels of communication with the aliens themselves in real time. [*TTSA already has plans for the necessary app.*] And to say that we will then be governed by "teaching authority" (a term taken from Roman Catholicism, the English translation of the Latin word *magisterium*) and "social science" instead of the military—democratic civil society apparently having disappeared long ago—this could only indicate a regime where social engineering has superseded all other forms of political power. (The social form envisioned would apparently resemble a 24/7 lineup of TED Talks with space aliens as the presenters.) Note also the retrospective reference to the social unrest and Spiritual Revolution of the 1960's, when "younger people expand(ed) their consciousness" as part of the CIA's most successful and far-reaching social engineering experiment to date: the mass dissemination of LSD throughout American society. This reference may be significant in view of the reappearance of controlled experimentation with psychedelics (now known as "entheogens") in American universities, along with the push to legalize them.

Robert Fleischer ends the episode by informing us: "If some government authority is telling us something about extraterrestrial beings visiting us on earth, you can be sure that it's not just because they want [the] whole [of] mankind to know about it. There must be another motivation behind this, and we don't know what this is." That Alien Disclosure is not simply disinterested but has an agenda behind it is entirely correct. It is not completely true, however, to say "we don't know what this is", since the general outline the likely agenda appears in this review.

Episode Six, "After Disclosure," begins with an ominous and cryptic statement:

> In the light of new facts published about the UFO phenomenon, the world is only a small step away from accepting a hitherto concealed truth: that we are not alone in the universe. It may be just a matter of months before the highest authorities have to look at the available

options to communicate this momentous message. It won't be easy. For six thousand years the pre-eminent life-form in the universe has been humanity. But what will the world face after Disclosure of the truth about UFOs?

Is the human race about to be ousted from its position of cosmic pre-eminence? If UFOs and their occupants have been with us for centuries if not millennia, as *Top Secret UFO Projects: Declassified* speculates, how could the mere announcement of their reality, which has certainly been accepted in one form or another by human beings at many points throughout our long history—certainly within the last 6000 years—so radically change our status? And where did the number "6000 years" come from? Modern anthropology has pushed the origin of the human race back millions of years, and recent archaeological discoveries have placed even the beginning of civilization at an substantially earlier date than 4000 BC. 6000 years is, precisely, the traditional age of the Earth, the period from the creation of Adam to the second coming of Christ, according to Judeo-Christianity; the famous Bishop Usher, calculating from scripture, placed the date of creation at 4004 BC. In other words, it is the *Judeo-Christian-Islamic dispensation*, and therefore the comic pre-eminence of Humanity as recognized by that dispensation [cf. Genesis 1:26–28; Q.33:72] that is destined to be overturned by the "Disclosure of the truth about UFOs." Once the "gods" have come back into human consciousness, belief in the God of the Abrahamic tradition will be no more. If this is not the announcement of a new religion, how else is such a declaration to be explained?

Now UFO researcher Alejandro Rojas tells us: "We

haven't, to my belief, had any overt hostile activity from any of these craft, so they could be observing; it could be that they are here to help us evolve. I think that there's numerous possibilities" [*GB*].

This is Big Lie Number One. After earlier episodes recounting horrific abductions, physical and psychological diseases caused by UFO encounters, the destruction of many aircraft etc., etc., we are expected to accept *this*? If you or I or Señor Rohas had perpetrated any of these atrocities, we would be arrested and charged as terror-ists—but the UFO aliens, like CIA assassins, apparently have immunity from prosecution. Some UFO Atrocity Deniers (UADs we could call them) may respond by claiming that the downed aircraft were only fired upon by UFOs after the aircraft fired first; their actions were entirely defensive. All reports agree, however, that UFOs are invulnerable to every human weapon that has been used against them; consequently the deaths of those pilots can only have been meant as acts of terror and a dire warning to the rest of us.

Next we must listen to Richard Dolan treating us to Big Lie Number Two: "What we can do is judge their actions," he says. "They are secretive, they are covert, they don't want to be known. So that's something that would make me wonder: why are they secretive?"

What?! After a huge fleet of UFOs buzzed the Capitol Building in Washington in 1952, as revealed in Episode One? After the numerous other incidents just recounted in the documentary, where they openly manifested their reality in no uncertain terms, even taking pains to deliber-ately attract our attention, sometimes in order to deliver urgent messages? *GB!* What possible reason could there be for issuing a contradiction so glaringly obvious that it alone is enough to totally destroy the credibility of the producers, writers and spokespeople of *Top Secret UFO Projects: Declassified?* The UFOs have always been conspicuous, often making no effort at all to conceal themselves—which they would be imminently capable of accomplishing due to their apparent ability to disappear entirely from view whenever they wish and speed invisibly from point to point. Their very erratic flight patterns can only be satisfactorily explained as attempts to attract human attention—not to mention their habit of parking in the middle of rural roads where they are virtually certain to encounter astounded motorists. In order to believe the people who made *Top Secret UFO Projects: Declassified* we must willingly destroy our own ability to think; apparently that's what they want.

Next the common "Ancient Aliens" meme makes its appearance, according to which the gods of all the archaic peoples were really ETs who have been "overseeing" the human race for millennia. The Native Americans are brought forward as experts and potential mentors to the rest of us in the art of ET-worship. The *kachinas* of the Pueblo tribes of the American Southwest, the "star people" of the Lakota and the "sky gods" of the Inuit are mentioned. The story of Lakota medicine man Wallace Black Elk from the Rosebud Reservation regarding his encounter with a UFO during a vision quest is recounted: "It was concave in shape; it was silent, but it was lit and luminesced like a neon light. These little people emerged from it . . . they could read minds and I could read their minds . . . so I welcomed them; I said: 'Welcome, welcome.'" Clifford Mahootć of the Zuñi tribe tells us more about them. He says:

> We believe that we were connected to the extraterrestrials from the beginning of what we call the Fourth World. They are the ones that are related to us . . . they gave us a connection to the other systems, like the star-systems . . . they are our teachers . . . they are actually our ancestors, because we took their DNA when they upgraded us . . . we took their teachings and they upgraded us through their efforts, using their particular, probably the DNA upgrades, and so in the long run we are part alien.

Apparently the Zuñis of today would be better described as "Zuñis 2.0." This is quite a unique and interesting doctrine for a First Nations people, revealing that the Zuñi tribe, and possibly other indigenous peoples in many parts of the world, must've already been practicing genetic engineering thousands of years ago. Perhaps these alien/human hybrids are actually the ancestors of the famous Skinwalkers of the Southwest; after all, anything is possible—isn't it? The documentary goes on to claim that the acceptance of the realty of UFO's and the "aliens" who pilot them is leading to "the reinterpretation of the myths, beliefs and faiths of indigenous peoples the world over." So instead of UFOs being explained according to the worldviews of the *indigenas*, those worldviews are being recast to bring them into line with the contemporary western belief in UFOs; this represents a mass hijacking and co-optation of the religions of the First Nations.

Next "the unwritten rule of non-interference in human affairs" is mentioned—perhaps unwritten but certainly not untelevised, since it is in fact the famous Prime Directive from the *Star Trek* TV series. The Prime Directive was *always* violated, of course—and anyone who believes that UFOs have not interfered in human affairs has never watched *Top Secret UFO Projects: Declassified.*

According to the research of UFO investigator Rey Hernandez, which sounds plausible but still needs confirmation, 84% of respondents to his survey—who were apparently all contactees—said that they wanted their ET appearances and contacts to continue. Initially, 30% viewed these experiences as negative, but this percentage decreased over time as the contacts continued. Apparently the initial horror is progressively overcome, and (as we can perhaps see with Travis Walton) an acceptance of the alien presence and message gradually takes its place. According to Hernandez, "for many of these beings, once you notice that you're scared, they phase out." For many others however, according to accounts included in the documentary, the reverse seems to be true: once they see that you're scared they go on scaring you, while ordering you not to be scared; this pretty much describes Travis Walton's experience.

Top Secret UFO Projects: Declassified generally interprets UFOs and their occupants as EBEs, extraterrestrial biological entities, though it also holds open the possibility, as Rey Hernandez tells us in this episode, that they may be psychic or "interdimensional" beings, rather than what we would consider to be normal material-plane astronauts. Nonetheless the documentary generally attributes their interdimensional abilities to their advanced state of technology—and it may finally prove true that highly advanced human technology will someday develop the power to open the door to other dimensions. Yet if a human being were to enter such a multi-dimensional world, body and soul, could he or she still be described as human? The subtle material region of the Intermediary or Psychic Plane, according to virtually all traditional accounts, is already thoroughly populated by beings with all the interdimensional talents you could wish for. Would a human immigrant to that world be welcomed as a naturalized "citizen," or would he, she or it, like some transhuman skinwalker, remain forever an interloper or a refugee there, straddling two worlds but at home in neither? Our proper home is earth, our proper form is human; the *Surah an-Naas*, the last surah of the Qur'an, warns us against the temptation to jettison the human form by following the suggestions of *the sneaking whisperer, who whispers in the hearts of Mankind, of the Jinn and of Mankind.* In the face of the growing intrusion of the UFO aliens into our world, "stay human" must become our mantra and our prayer—as should become clear as soon as we understand the *doctrine* that *Top Secret UFO Projects: Declassified* does its best to impress upon us.

Finally the endgame of the documentary begins to take shape. The Narrator says: "Disclosure of the secrets concerning the activities of aliens on Earth, and declassification by the military and intelligence agencies about UFO encounters, will undoubtedly be a revolutionary turning-point in human history." He goes on to speculate that the aliens will likely introduce new ideas relating to conservation, social inequality and advanced technology, and asks whether or not the human race is ready for these developments—to which Mary Rodwell replies: "I think that it's going to be a very big shock to a lot of people, particularly if they're very entrenched in the paradigm of today, *particularly with religion*" [we see a brief shot of a swinging church bell as if to signal: *ding-dong, good-bye*].

In the place of the old religious paradigm, the Aliens will bring a "religion" and a theology of their own, one that promises great rewards to those who have faith in it. We are told that the ETs will likely apply their "human technologies", notably genetic engineering, to eliminating most of the diseases that plague humanity. They will also solve our environmental crisis and overcome social inequality; therefore any failure to believe in them and welcome them will be virtually suicidal. According to Mary Rodwell, people will be very angry when they realize that the suppression of Disclosure has delayed the appearance of these saving technologies; in other words, the failure of governments and militaries to disclosed what they know about extraterrestrials is (it is implied) nothing less than a crime against humanity, a crime against which the People will rise up to exact their just revenge. Under whose leadership, we may ask, will this world revolution take place? And even before this happens, will the day come when Congress passes a bill defining all criticism of Extraterrestrials as illegal "hate speech"? We shall see.

The Aliens are here to advance human evolution and human awareness; they will raise the consciousness of the human race to a higher level where greed, war and selfishness will no longer be motivations. Some of the central dogmas of the emerging *Extraterrestrial Theology*, according to the narrator and six UFO "experts," are as follows:

MICHAEL P. MASTERS: If consciousness isn't bound by spacetime, there could be some aspect of that that relates to this phenomenon, there could be communication across different points in time, information-exchange between those who are more or open to it or aware of it or have those abilities. [Clearly a higher spiritual caste is being posited here.]

RICHARD DOLAN: A lot of UFO sightings seem to be connected with our own consciousness, our own mind, and I will never be able to get rid of that idea...

ROBERT FLEISCHER: This huge consciousness that we are talking about, is this possibly the universe itself, is this God, and we are part of It? Those are very profound questions, and I think that once the UFO subject has been freed from the ridicule factor, scientists and philosophers will be able to start to tackle those questions.

KEVIN DAY (naval air intercept controller during the Nimitz Encounters): I got the impression they could read our minds...

NARRATOR: Acknowledgement of the potential for extrasensory perception, telepathy and other abilities would constitute a radical turn-around by the scientific world. For the moment, however, this world is unwilling to listen, to accept that these abilities may have emerged as a result of extraterrestrial encounters.

MARY RODWELL: We have their DNA. We are, if you like, an intelligently designed species with perhaps as much as twelve different species' of non-human intelligence with their DNA...

This last dogma seems designed to co-opt the emerging information-theory-based theology of Intelligent Design, pioneered by Philip Johnson, William Dembski, Michael

Behe and others, by rejecting an intelligent Divine Creator in favor of a committee of Extraterrestrials, who are actually our real creators via genetic engineering. (As for the question of who designed our designers, and who designed the designers of our designers, in an infinite regression back to God knows what, this immediately invalidating objection is never dealt with.) And not only are we creatures of the aliens, we are not really even human beings at all, just an amalgam of heterogeneous genome-fragments from many different species. By this ingeniously-conceived attack on the human form the producers of *Top Secret UFO Projects: Declassified* have disallowed the Christian doctrine of the Incarnation, the Islamic doctrine of the prophethood of Adam, the Hindu doctrine of the avatars of Vishnu, the Buddhist doctrine of "the human state hard-to-attain," and the Hebrew/Kabbalistic doctrine of the Adam Kadmon, all at one stroke. Christ could not be True God and True Man if there is no such thing as True Man! By this we know that the ET religion has been designed (though not entirely by ETs!) to supersede and invalidate all the traditional religions of the Earth. And as for how these various commentators are so certain of what they know, only those of little faith will dare to ask such a shameful and invalidating question, because—*they know,* man, *they know!*

That we are expected to worship—or if not worship, then at least place our hopes in—beings the documentary visually presents as horrible walking corpses, blanched, naked and skeletal, lacking genitals, with bloated heads and enormous jet black eyes, is outrageous and insulting, though certainly not uncommon. If we imagine, despite all evidence to the contrary, that they might be here to help us, then why doesn't the documentary present them as august beings in long white robes, or wise interstellar ambassadors in silver jumpsuits, like Michael Rennie in *The Day the Earth Stood Still*, which would be just as true to the many forms in which the aliens appear as the famous "grays" popularized by Whitley Strieber? Possibly because, in today's world, such an image would be neither plausible nor *attractive* to the majority of the people likely to respond to it. If you can get people to react with positive feelings to images of ugliness, you have damaged their ability to discern and respond to beauty; likewise, if you can induce them to accept obviously contradictory statements without noticing the contradiction, you have wounded their ability to recognize the truth.

✳

Whether we will be ultimately treated to "the world must unite against the alien menace" or "the world must unite under its benevolent alien overlords" remains to be seen; maybe we'll get a little of both. A common meme in contemporary culture—and not just in video games—is that of "the good demons vs. the bad demons" (i.e., Gog vs. Magog), which effectively acts to co-opt and negate the idea of an ultimate conflict between Good and Evil. *Good* does not really exist, of course, since everybody's idea of the Good is different; the more realistic view is to accept that all choices and conflicts are between the greater and the lesser of two evils—which means, of course, that Evil is the basic principle of Reality, while "the Good" is nothing but a wish-fulfillment fantasy, a pipe-dream, an archaic superstition believed in only by bigots and religious fanatics. It is widely-pervasive beliefs such as this that are re-casting "post-Christian" society in overtly Luciferian terms.

As for the question of "Why Disclosure Now?" that many have asked, I can think of three answers: 1) The Clandestine Disclosurite Elite have decided, according to whatever criteria they accept as valid, that the populace is now finally sufficiently conditioned to be ripe for Full Disclosure; 2) Global tensions between the western world and China and/or Russia, not to mention the climate disaster and the U.S. capitulation to the Jihadists in Central Asia, have reached a point of unparalleled crisis where the Disclosurites feel they must play their long-anticipated Global Unity Card as fast as possible before it's too late; 3) They, like the rest of us who have been following the UFO enigma, just couldn't take the suspense any longer, which means that they were finally unable to resist moving their 50-year or 70-year social engineering project into its endgame: *Time to go for broke! Time to announce the advent of the New Global Religion! Time to flush the Aliens out of the closet as the literal gods of the New World Order!* Fortunately for this study, their over-eagerness to bring their whole paradigm-shift agenda into its terminal phase has apparently resulted in a fatal lack of caution on their part, a violation of the limits of necessary discretion—which is to say that they have tipped their hand, let the cat out of the bag. Our vigilant little watchdog has pulled the curtain aside to reveal the Wizard operating the levers of the global matrix, which (God willing) could mean that he and his assistants will soon be forced to board their escape balloon, or saucer, and beat a hasty retreat—unless Divine Justice requires that they be given time to perfect the Ultimate Lie so it can be exposed and obliterated by the Ultimate Truth and Reality, at the coming of the Hour. (And God knows best.)

In conclusion, I do not claim to have absolutely proved that any single claim or incident in *Top Secret UFO Projects: Declassified* is false. What I have proved, beyond any reasonable doubt, is that the documentary is filled with deliberately contradictory statements that are so outrageous, and so obvious, that they make it impossible for any rational human being to take it seriously—except as a transparent attempt to manipulate and deceive.

Mythic Afterword

The following legendary narrative will only mean something to those who are well versed in world scripture, myth and folklore, and who also accept that accounts of the Fairies, the Jinn, the gods, the angels and the Deity represent realities of a non-material order, not simply human beliefs. It is largely my own speculation, though it is nonetheless in line with certain passages in the Qur'an—and since the military and the CIA are not above manufacturing a myth for the masses to believe in, I thought I would try my hand at the same game. I hasten to add that the following speculation is in no way orthodox Muslim doctrine, nor does it explicitly appear anywhere in the Qur'an. It was suggested to me by the theme from world mythology which, in its Greek rendition, appears as the fall of the Titans, who are analogous to the Norse Giants and the Hindu Asuras; interestingly enough, one of the names in pre-Islamic Arabic legend for a certain tribe of the Jinn is *al-Asr*.

That said, it is mythopoetically possible to imagine that the Jinn—which can be taken as a general term for the *daimones* or denizens of the Psychic or Intermediary Plane, who assume innumerable forms, whether demonic, benevolent or neutral—were once the "central" or "axial" beings for this terrestrial world. In Qur'anic terms, they possessed the *Amana*, the Trust, a God-given duty to act as His vice-regents on Earth [cf. Q. 41:53], but they forfeited this Trust at one point, after which it passed to Humanity. This would explain the refusal, recounted in the Qur'an, of Iblis (who was to become the Muslim Satan) to obey Allah's command to bow down to Adam, in the timeless time before the First Man was sent down from heaven to govern the terrestrial plane [Q. 2:29]. Iblis was a Jinn placed among the angels, just as the Norse god Loki was a giant, a member of the *Jötun*, placed among the *Aesir*, the gods; most likely he refused to prostrate to Adam out of envy, because he resented the fact that he had been demoted in Adam's favor. ("The Envier" mentioned in the *Surah al-Falaq* is, precisely, Iblis.) The *Amana* was progressively lost by the Jinn over a long period of time due to various transgressions, earlier in some geographical areas than others. For example, after the advent of the Abrahamic religions in the Near East, under whose dispensation God spoke directly to man through the prophets, the Jinn lost their role as intermediaries between the Celestials (the angels or "gods") and Humankind [cf. Q. 72: 8–10], whereas in the New World, the faithful and obedient among the western hemisphere Jinn—whom the Hopis call the *Kachinas*—by-and-large continued to fulfill that function.

In our age, however, those religions in which God speaks directly to man through the prophets have become weakened, due to the lateness of the hour and the fast-approaching end of the present cycle-of-manifestation. Sensing this weakness, the disinherited Jinn, who are generally analogous to the pagan gods, have vowed that they will supplant the "usurper" Man, re-take the throne of terrestrial existence, and re-assume the Trust—forgetting that this Trust cannot be "conquered," only *entrusted* by God to whomever He will. These rebellious Jinn are the beings who are presently appearing to us as the "aliens" or "extra-terrestrials"; and, as *Top Secret UFO Projects: Declassified* makes all too clear, their agenda includes the overthrow of the revealed religions and the installation of themselves as the new "gods" to be worshipped by humanity. These beings falsely claim to be worthy of such worship because of the evolving myth that it was they, not Almighty God, who created us; this is the central deception they are laboring to enforce. However, the remnant of the legitimate Earth Guardians of an earlier world age are in no way to be identified with the despised and rejected rebels who, through pride and disobedience, lost their title to that role in this one; only malignant reprobates and supreme fools like these would ever dare to attempt to usurp the prerogatives of the Creator! Consequently, since the Zuñis know the Mother/Father God Awonawilona as the Creator of all things, when Clifford Mahooté claims we were created by the space aliens instead he is falsifying and perverting Zuñi belief. And as for Wallace Black Elk,

Janet McCloud, an elder of the Nisqually nation, says this in the article "Spiritual Hucksterism: The Rise of the Plastic Medicine Men" by Ward Churchill: "We've got our . . . Wallace Black Elks and others who'd sell their own mother if they thought it would turn a quick buck. What they're selling isn't theirs to sell, and they know it. They're thieves and sellouts, and they know that too. That's why you never see them around Indian people anymore. When we have our traditional meetings and gatherings, you never see . . . those sorts showing up." [https://www.culturalsurvival.org/publications/cultural-su rvival-quarterly/spiritual-hucksterismthe-rise-plastic-medicine-men]

Episode Six of *Top Secret UFO Projects: Declassified* reports, quite accurately, that the many of the "aliens" who abduct human beings in our time say that they are now appearing to us to warn us against actions that could destroy all life on Earth, which they and other sentient beings in the universe recognize as a terrestrial paradise, now sadly on its last legs. (Emery Smith goes so far as to call our planet "the Disneyland of the Universe.") This is why, for example, they appear above nuclear missile installations and demonstrate their power to disrupt them and shut them down. I generally accept this account as accurate. However, their actual reason for being alarmed at human destructiveness is much less idealistic: it's simply that they live here too, and they recognize that Humanity now has the power to destroy the Earth as a home for both men and Jinn. They are not extraterrestrials but "intraterrestrials," inhabiting the region where the Psychic Plane intersects the subtle-material dimension of the Physical Plane (which is not to say that they couldn't be in contact with other worlds beyond Earth, whether physical or subtle, through their own channels). This explains their ability, accepted by both Allen Hynek and Jacques Vallee, to affect both our minds and the material environment. Unfortunately, however, their entirely legitimate desire to moderate human destructiveness is corrupted by their ambition to regain the position of earthly pre-eminence that the Creator took away from them long ago—six thousand years ago, according to Episode Six. "The only way to control these unruly and destructive human beings," they reason, "is to make them our slaves." This, however, is something that the Creator will not allow.

Appendices

I
Speculations on the Future Development of the UFO/ Alien Myth

II
Invocation Against the Alien Temptation

✸

APPENDIX I

Speculations on the Future Development of the UFO/Alien Myth

Jonathan Michael Solvie

This analysis, which I received just as the present book was about to go to print, has the virtue of being relevant and insightful whether we see the "Aliens" as mythic entities invented to play a part in mass social engineering theater, or as actual preternatural beings inhabiting the subtle-corporeal realm who are now mounting an increasingly powerful insurgency into our world, either via arcane technology or by their own inherent capacities. Either way, whether the ETs are fictional or factual or both, they are already having a profound effect on the global worldview of the human race.

DEAR CHARLES:

I suggest that you keep a watchful eye on the "Nordics" ("tall blonds," etc.), for I strongly suspect that these may come to play a more central role than perhaps any other "race" (whether their outward mask is true to their real form is always an important question and shouldn't be naively accepted on face-value) in the New World Order, as far as the "New World Religion" is concerned, at any rate. [NOTE: *The Nordics are one of the various Alien races in UFO mythology.*] The most widespread visualization of "UFO Alien" today is of course the "Grey." (We all know that look.) But in terms of alien beings presenting themselves as benevolent teachers of New Age truth, the tall Whites of more or less human appearance (somewhat reminiscent of Tolkien's Elves, that elder race) seem to predominate as the preeminent "messengers" *par excellence.* And when it comes to the "good alien vs. bad alien" conflict theater the social engineers may orchestrate, the meme has already been around for decades that these Whites (referred to by various names) are at least for the most part on the good side, noble and enlightened (although there is the occasional admission that there may exist a "rogue faction" which aided the Nazis, etc.).

I think the "Nordics" (we're only talking of those actively intervening as part of the UFO show, of course) are the most perfect agents of Luciferian deception, for all their fair appearance. I think all the focus on "Greys," "Reptilians" and so on may even serve as a distraction and diversion from the more central role to be played by the "Whites" in the deception. I wonder if these "Whites" (whatever their true identity may be; if they are cold soulless psychopaths, it wouldn't be wrong even to name them "Reptilians"—serpents—regardless of the appearance of the mask) may finally arrive with great strength on the visible global scene as the major player and highest authority of all the races of the "Federation" *after* humanity has been intimidated, scared and alienated by the "Greys" and perhaps other less appealing players, offering relief and "spirituality." This is at least one possibility. The game can play out in many different ways, and I'm not an insider, so I don't know what is planned. But think about it, Charles: humanity was created in the image and likeness of God, right? Or, as the One World Religion will perhaps correct it: "of the *gods*." And which of the races appearing as part of the UFO show do literally have a physical appearance similar to humanity (but more "perfect")? You guessed it, the "Nordics." It is *they* who will probably be starred in the role of the returning *Annunaki*. It all fits.

You probably know about Michael Salla in the Disclosure Movement? I think many particular details of the theater show they are preparing can be gleaned from the works of this disinformation agent. Watch this powerful propaganda film worthy of Goebbels and Riefenstahl, "Antarctica and Origins of the Dark Fleet," whose theme is the survival of the Nazis in Antarctica, their alliance with the evil aliens, and the later reluctant alliance of the United States with these forces after the defeat of our air force by the Nazi flying saucers [https://youtu.be/L1fcc6 YaFlA].

In Salla's propaganda works, which he claims to be based on intelligence from insider sources, a recurring theme is once again the "Nordics" starred in the role of good guys, allied to the "good" faction of the deep state, the "white hats"—that stupid disinfo myth which many Trump-supporters were conned by. On the side of the *Bad* deep state faction on the other hand, which includes the Nazi International with headquarters in underground Antarctica, we are presented with the "Reptilians," made infamous by David Icke and others. The Nordic/Reptilian conflict appears in "History of the Extraterrestrial Agenda & the Coming Global Revolution" in which Donald

Trump figures prominently [https://www.youtube.com/
watch?v=o7pnd-nXGPs], another example of the kind of
insidious propaganda Dr. Salla's group is responsible for.

But now let me point out to you something which I
think indicates knowing deception: Why does Salla hardly
mention the tall "Whites" in connection with the Nazis,
when he *does* focus on the witches of the *Vril Gesellschaft*,
an element of the occult inner circle of the Third Reich, as
contactees receiving the instructions for new revolutionary
technology? For these witches, as far as we know, claimed
to be in contact with beings similar to the "Nordics,"
which certainly coincides with the Nazi obsession with a
blond "Aryan" master-race, the *Übermenschen*. (The secret
society I just mentioned was even named after the British
occult "initiate" Bulwer-Lytton's coded novel *Vril: The
Coming Race* which describes exactly this type of alien
race.) Why does Salla soft-pedal Nazi involvement with
the "Nordics" when they play such a prominent part in his
mythology? Clearly he (and others) would ideally have
liked to cover up that connection entirely and focus only
on "the Reptilians." My own speculation is that the "Nor-
dic rogue faction" theory is *damage control* in view of the
fact that the involvement of the tall Whites with the Nazis
is, if not a solidly established historical fact in this field of
research, at least an old and well known story in UFO
mythology.

A note on conspiracy researcher David Icke, whom I
mentioned in passing. After being in close contact with
him I have good reasons to believe that he is not only an
intelligence asset and disinfo agent, tasked with cultivating a controlled opposition, but possibly also a conscious

counter-initiate. This is really quite transparent if you study recent video material featuring him. It is funny how he likes to use promotional photos of himself now in which he tries to look as evil, sinister and intimidating as possible. Hidden in plain sight. Anyway, in Icke's propaganda material, too, which recently has increasingly taken on the trappings of neo-Gnosticism (Archons, the God of the Bible as evil demiurge, the historical, incarnated Jesus as false fiction, etc.), he continues to go on about the "Reptilians, Reptilians, Reptilians" and also the "Greys" as evil alien players of the conspiracy, but—strangely—virtually *nothing* about the tall "Whites." He does absolutely *nothing* to prepare his followers for the possibility of a coming spiritual deception on part of the fair, appealing "Nordics," even though *he must certainly know* about the data in support of such a conclusion. After all, he has himself stated in several contexts that the New Age movement is deceptive (although he is himself arguably part of it). So again, why this taboo, even in the case of Icke? Could it be that he doesn't want us to mentally associate the Nordics with other intrusive alien races because he is setting the stage for their unexpected appearance as our saviors from the Reptilians and the Greys?

APPENDIX II

Invocation Against
the Alien Temptation

Satan is the Ape of God—
But since Man is made in the Image and likeness of
   God
It is also true to say that Satan is the Ape of Man;
This is something we are now seeing in the UFO
   phenomenon.
Christ appeared as a Man, not as an animal or a star
   or a robot;
According to the Holy Qur'an, the *Amana* or Trust—
The station of Guardian of the Earth in the Name of
   the Creator—
Was given to Man, not to the "heavens, the earth and
   the hills," the non-sentient elements;
Likewise the Buddhists maintain that it is only from
   "the human state hard-to attain" that Perfect
   Total Enlightenment can be gained.
The UFO aliens, also known as the *kafir* Jinn, are
   now working hard to make us forget this;
That's why the *Surah an-Naas* or "Humanity," the last
   surah of the Qur'an
Came to the Prophet Muhammad, peace and blessing
   be upon him
In the form of an invocation against this last tempta-
   tion—
The temptation to renounce the human form:

Bismillah al-Rahman al-Rahim,
Qul:
"A'uzu bi-rabbin Naas
Malikin Naas
Ilaahin Naas
Min sharril waswaasil khan Naas
Allazii yuwaswisu fii sudurin Naas
Minal Jinnati wan Naas."

In the Name of Allah, the Beneficent, the
    Merciful,
        Say:
"I take refuge in the Lord of Mankind
The King of Mankind
The God of Mankind
From the evil of the sneaking Whisperer
Who whispereth in the hearts of Mankind
Of the Jinn and of Mankind."